Coaching Pattern-Read Coverage

Tom Olivadotti

ISBN: 978-1-60679-046-5
Library of Congress Control Number: 2009922600
Cover design: Studio J Art & Design
Book layout: Studio J Art & Design
Front cover photo: Doug Benc/Getty Images

Coaches Choice
P.O. Box 1828
Monterey, CA 93942
www.coacheschoice.com

Dedication

To my dear wife, whose patience, understanding, and support have allowed me to put maximum effort into the coaching profession; to my two children, who are my biggest supporters; and to my three grandchildren, this book is to remember their granddad.

Acknowledgments

To every coach I have worked with during the last 40 years. I have learned so much from every one of you.

Contents

Introduction

In modern day football, it will not suffice for defenders to drop to particular points on the field because offenses have receivers running option routes (i.e., "get open routes") to get away from defenders in zone coverages. Finding receivers in pass routes certainly is not new; players have been doing it on their own for years. This book outlines a pattern reading defensive system based on those practices.

A great pass rush can make a team's coverages look better than they really are. However, if a team has an average pass rush, then pattern reading can make the quarterback hold the ball a second longer to aid the pass rush.

I have used pattern reading since I was a high school coach. In the past, it was not as extensive as it has become in some of today's football. I began to believe in pattern reading because I did not like easy completions and did not have an answer for certain patterns. "Hustle to it" is not a sufficient strategy for breaking up 10-yard completions. In contrast, pattern reading provides ways to tell players exactly how they should cover a play.

Much depends on what you believe and your philosophy in zone coverages. The success of pattern reading will depend on what you teach in the progression (i.e., early depth in the drop or quick recognition to limit depth) (refer to Chapter 12 for teaching progression). Teaching points on the field drop is much easier in the early stages of installation; eventually, however, reading coverage must be brought into the teaching. These strategies are important to the success of pattern reading. General coverage points and general terms are discussed in the early chapters of this book.

Ultimately, pattern reading is the ability to outnumber the offense to the side of the throw based on the route being executed (e.g., four defenders on three receivers). It is accomplished in an aggressive manner by breaking on receivers' patterns to allow the defender to get closer to the ball. Hopefully, this book provides a starting point for teaching pattern reading with information that will stimulate your thinking.

How important is pass defense in modern football?

Years ago, the playoff teams in the NFL were in the upper echelon in the statistical category of yards per *rush* against defense. However, in the 2007 season, the most interesting statistic occurred: all 12 playoff teams were the top 12 statistically in yards per pass against defense (Figure 1). This finding demonstrates the importance of an incomplete pass.

Team	Rank for Total Yards	Rank for Rush Average	Rank for Pass Average	Rank for Yards Per Play	Rank for Points Allowed Per Game	Rank for Sacks Per Play	Total Takeaways
New England	4	26	5	7	4	2	31
Pittsburgh	1	14	1	3	2	15	25
Tennessee	5	15	3	5	8	10	34
Indianapolis	3	6	4	2	1	26	37
San Diego	14	17 (tie)	8	13	5	7	48
Jacksonville	12	17 (tie)	11	17	10	12	30
Dallas	9	13	7	6	13	5	29
New York Giants	7	9	10	8	17	1	25
Washington	8	3	6	4	11	27	24
Tampa Bay	2	7	2	1	3	14	35
Seattle	15	12	9	9	6T	4	34
Green Bay	11	11	12	12	6T	13	28

Figure 1. 2007 NFL playoffs team statistics

What It All Means to Making the Playoffs

- Total yards: All playoff teams were in the top half.
- Rush average (biggest change): Only four of the 12 playoff teams were in the top 10.
- Pass average (biggest surprise): All 12 playoff teams were the top 12 teams in yards per pass; this statistic is critical to making the playoffs.
- Yards per play: Nine of the 12 playoff teams were in the top 10 (San Diego, Green Bay, and Jacksonville were not in the top 10). Baltimore was the only nonplayoff team in the top 10.
- Points allowed per game: Only three playoff teams were not in the top 10; only one team (New York Giants) was not in the upper half.

- Sacks per play: The Super Bowl teams were ranked 1 and 2, but the playoff teams were not all that good. Only six of the 12 playoff teams were in the top 10.
- Takeaways: The average for all 32 NFL teams was 28. The average for nine of the 12 playoff teams was 28 or greater. If giveaways and takeaways are summarized, then only three playoff teams were not on the plus side (Tennessee, Washington, and New York Giants).

Counting and Identifying

It is important for the defense to know how to identify receivers in pattern progression. In the count method, #1 to #5 refer to strong to weak receivers from the outside in. The receivers could be numbered as #1, #2, and #3 strong or #1, #2, and #3 weak; however, for the purposes of this book, #1 to #5 with #5 being the first weakside receiver will be used. It is impossible to discuss pattern reading without this identification process.

Receiver Numbering

The receivers are numbered from the outside in (Diagram 1-1). They are referred to as #1, #2, #3, # 4, and #5 strong to weak. In teaching pattern progression, it does not matter who the receivers are; only the final number that they are positioned matters. Diagram 1-2 shows final numbering of receivers after the snap. Numbering can change on a "quick switch" by receivers. Diagram 1-3 illustrates another example of a final count of receivers.

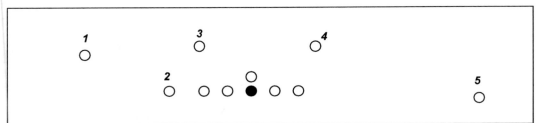

Diagram 1-1. Numbering of receivers from the outside in

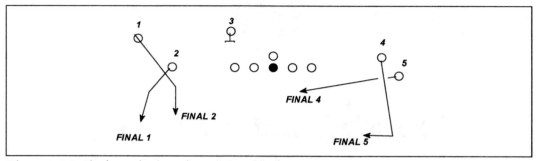

Diagram 1-2. Final numbering of receivers after the snap

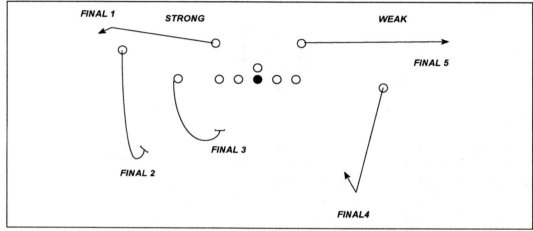

Diagram 1-3. Another example of a final count of receivers

Importance of the #3 Receiver

Knowing the final location of the #3 receiver after the snap dictates how and where the help is for the rest of the hook/curl defenders (Diagram 1-4). This information determines which side to "push" toward (for the defender). It also determines how the defender away from the #3 receiver will play his zone coverage. Once players master the technique, it becomes easy.

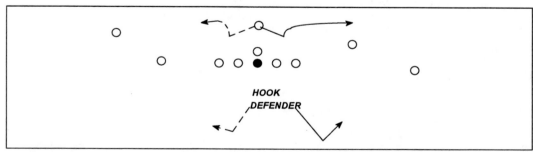

Diagram 1-4. Final location of the #3 receiver

Four Strong Receivers

When four receivers are on the strongside, it is called "flow." Flow can occur by action after the snap of the ball (Diagram 1-5) or by alignment (Diagram 1-6). Why is it important? Flow tells the backside defender where to push the zone coverage. It prevents him from "covering air."

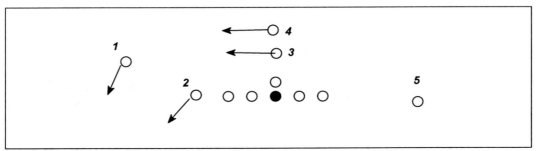

Diagram 1-5. Flow by action

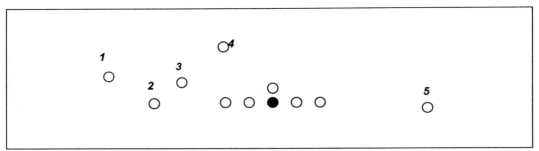

Diagram 1-6. Flow by alignment

Three Weak Receivers

When three receivers are on the weakside, it is called "flood." Flood can occur by action (Diagram 1-7) or by alignment (Diagram 1-8).

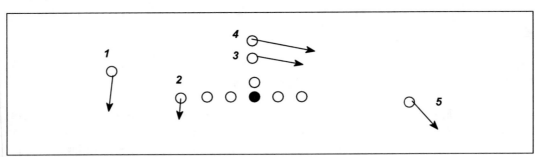

Diagram 1-7. Flood by action

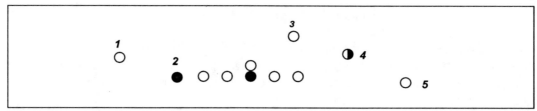

Diagram 1-8. Flood by alignment

Dropback (Split Action)

When three receivers are on the strongside and two receivers are on the weakside, it is considered dropback. Dropback can occur by action (Diagram 1-9) or by alignment (Diagram 1-10).

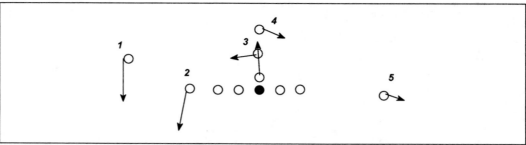

Diagram 1-9. Dropback by action

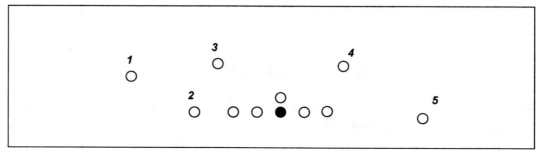

Diagram 1-10. Dropback by alignment

Empty Sets

Formations with no backs will be classified as flow, flood, or dropback. Of course, some unusual things will occur, especially with motion by the offense. Empty sets sometimes are good for defensive recognition, such as showing defensive responsibilities before the snap of the ball.

Formation Identification

Basically, formations are broken down into the following four categories:

- Two-back set: In this formation, two backs are in the backfield; it is a two-back look. A wideout may be in the backfield, but it is still a two-back look to start. Movement may change the look. Diagram 1-11 shows the finished formation.
- 2-2 set (one back in the backfield): In this formation, two receivers are to either side of the center (Diagram 1-12).
- Trips set (one back in the backfield): In this formation, three receivers are to one side, and one receiver is to the weakside (Diagram 1-13).
- Empty set (no backs in the backfield): In this formation, three receivers could be to one side, and two receivers could be to the other side. In addition, four receivers could be to one side (quads), and one receiver could be to the weakside. With no backs in the backfield, only two possibilities exist (Diagrams 1-14 and 1-15).

Note: Although the term "back" is used, the receiver could be of any type (e.g., a wideout).

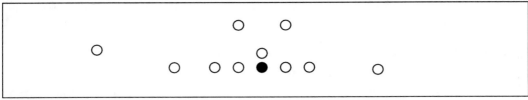

Diagram 1-11. A two-back look regardless of personnel

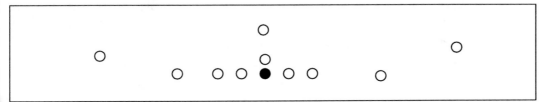

Diagram 1-12. A 2-2 set with one back in the backfield (neutral or offset)

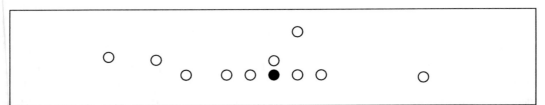

Diagram 1-13. Trips set with one back in the backfield (neutral or offset)

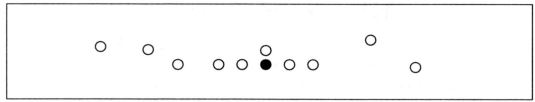

Diagram 1-14. Empty (3-2) set with no backs in the backfield

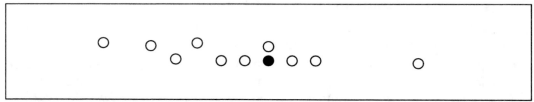

Diagram 1-15. Empty (quads) set with no backs in the backfield

Defender Labeling

Because defensive positions will first be discussed without labeling specific coverages (refer to Chapter 7 for labeling specific coverages), the technique of the dropper will be identified as opposed to a name on a position (i.e., linebacker, safety, etc.). This strategy will allow you to "plug" in the position you deem necessary to fit into your specific defense. Following are the terms used to identify the defenders:

- *Hook defender (H)*: He will cover 5 to 15 yards deep, including any route coming inside; the preliminary drop starts inside the #2, #3, and #4 receivers.
- *Hook/curl defender (HC)*: He has the same responsibilities as the hook defender but will also carry the seam route (the seam is any route inside the numbers straight downfield; it is also called the curl/seam when applying it to two deep).
- *Flat defender (F)*: He will cover any threat to the outside towards the sideline.
- *Deep-third defender (C)*: He will cover the deep outside one-third of the field.
- *Deep-half defender (DH)*: He will cover the deep half of the field to his side.
- Deep-middle defender (M): He will cover the deep middle of the field.
- *Short- to deep-cover defender (Q)*: He will cover one-quarter of the field, usually from the numbers to the middle of the field.

Any symbol or name can be assigned to the defenders. Specific aiming points are limited in width because the routes will bring the defender to the receiver. Starting points will be attached to specific coverages (refer to Chapters 7 through 9). Defensive personnel may change (nickel and dime), but the zones will not change. For this reason, zone droppers are identified by the zones they will drop into; the defensive personnel can be interchanged.

2

What Is Pattern Reading?

Pattern reading is the ability to play aggressive zone defensive coverage. It decreases the holes and seams in a zone pass defense. Pattern reading puts a defender on a tight man-to-man coverage on a receiver after the pass pattern expresses itself. Hook/curl defenders are used most often in pattern reading. Pattern reading puts a defender on a hook/curl drop based on where the receiver is located rather than a specific drop to a reference point on the field. An initial aiming point is based on the coverage, but the depth and angle on the rest of the pass drop are based on the location of the receiver's route.

Diagrams 2-1 and 2-2 show a hook/curl defender (who could be a linebacker or defensive back based on the defense called) dropping to the receiver. The drop is not predetermined to a point on the field (after the initial aiming point). He may have to turn his back to get in the throwing lane and to locate the receiver once he is an arm's distance from the receiver; he must then look back to the quarterback.

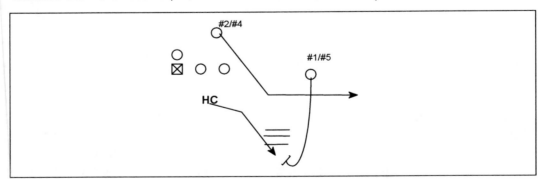

Diagram 2-1. Hook/curl defender dropping to the receiver

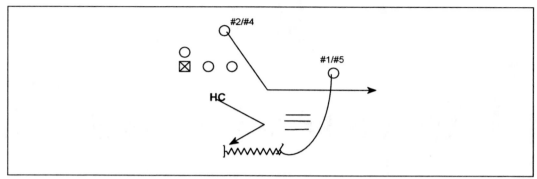

Diagram 2-2. Hook/curl defender dropping to the receiver

This strategy goes against the premise of a player never turning his back on the quarterback. With better quarterbacks and higher levels of competition, the throwing lanes in zone coverage must be eliminated and the receiver(s) must be found. How many times have you seen receivers slide in or out on option routes to get open? The defender is looking back to the quarterback and loses sight of the receiver (Diagram 2-3), and the pass is completed easily. Good quarterbacks find holes in zones. Good quarterbacks do not stare down target receivers early in coverage. Therefore, reading quarterbacks early in coverage is a moot point. The defender should have an early aiming point (i.e., 12 to 15 yards inside the hash mark, which is just the beginning of the drop). This strategy gives the defender an early angle to the receiver.

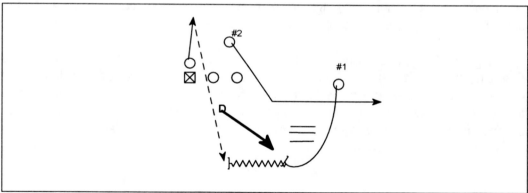

Diagram 2-3. A defender looking back at the quarterback and losing the receiver

Tight zone coverage should be used instead of man-to-man coverage because it allows defenders to get a jump on routes with underneath defenders helping inside. It eliminates one-on-one coverages. It allows tight coverage after the pattern expresses itself. Defenders are coming up to receivers instead of catching up to them in man-to-man coverage. It also helps an inferior player to get a jump on routes.

Keying a Receiver (Five Reads)

In any coverage, the hook/curl defender will have a receiver who he must key to determine the angle and/or depth of his drop based on the action of the key (receiver). The key can only do five actions: across, hold, inside, outside, or seam (straight) (Diagram 2-4). The seam route is defined as any route inside the numbers straight downfield. No route is more dangerous for allowing big plays against the defense. It is not a hard throw for the quarterback. Seams must always be accounted for in coverages. Each action by the key will dictate the angle and width of the pass drop after the defender's initial drop and/or the coverage called, which becomes part of the teaching progression.

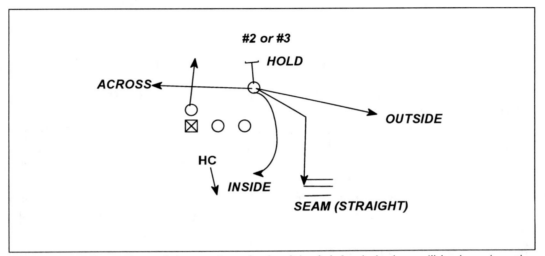

Diagram 2-4. Five actions of the receiver; the hook/curl defender's drop will be based on the coverage called.

Leading and Trailing Players

Leading and trailing are terms used when a defender in zone coverage picks up a receiver who is closest to him in his zone coverage, while the defender who is away from him will pick up a receiver in the zone based on the coverage of the first defender when zones are identified. Basically, zones change based on the routes of the receivers, which applies most to hook/curl defenders. Diagrams 2-5 and 2-6 show how a hook drop can vary based on the receiver with the other defender covering for the lead defender. The first defender picks up the first hook defender who is in his "face," and the trail defender plays off the lead defender. Two hook receivers are at different locations in each diagram. The lead and trail defenders help the coverage by playing off each other.

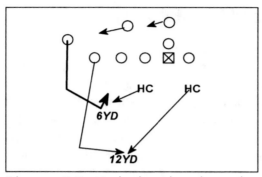

Diagram 2-5. Hook drop based on the receiver with the other defender covering for the lead defender (example 1)

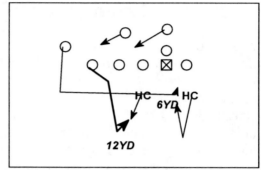

Diagram 2-6. Hook drop based on the receiver with the other defender covering for the lead defender (example 2)

Flat Defenders Avoiding Covering Air

The technique of flat coverage in pattern reading demonstrates how to avoid covering air, which is different from "buzzing the flat." The technique for a flat defender is a drop about 12 yards deep inside the widest receiver's original position. The drop technique will be at a 45-degree angle outside with the head on a "swivel." The flat defender will maintain leverage on the widest receiver. Inside or outside leverage will depend on the coverage called. Basically, the flat defender will slide inside with the widest receiver; he will never turn his back on the quarterback. The flat defender should never cross a receiver. He must stay as wide as the widest receiver from inside the #2, #3, and #4 receivers (Diagrams 2-7 to 2-10). The flat defender should try to force a cushion through the curl area to the flat area.

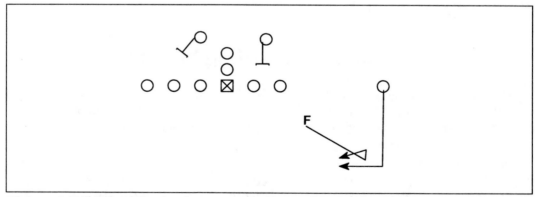

Diagram 2-7. The flat defender does not cover air. He slides inside with the receiver but never crosses the widest receiver.

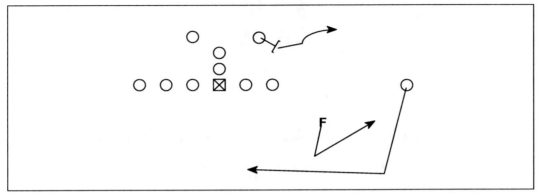

Diagram 2-8. The receiver crosses the flat defender's face, and he must cover the threat.

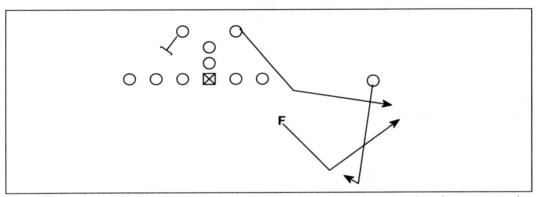

Diagram 2-9. An immediate threat to the flat forces the flat defender to be alert to go to the flat on the throw by the passer.

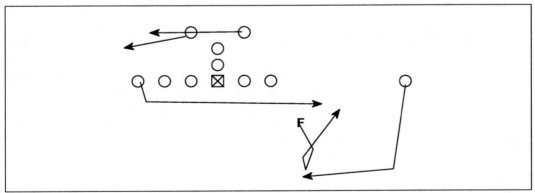

Diagram 2-10. Flow: The flat defender must not allow a receiver to cross his face to the flat.

3

Terms, Techniques, and Communication

The techniques and terms used in reading patterns must be understood to discuss this concept. The calls and techniques are used in all defenses in some way. The nomenclature may be different, but the meaning is the same.

Drop Points and Aiming Points

Every zone coverage has a starting point in regard to the depth and width of the defender's drop. When pattern reading, the width and depth of the drop will vary based on the receivers' routes. In normal zone coverage, a defender will drop to points on the field regardless of the receivers' routes (refer to Chapter 4 for a discussion on this topic).

Individual Drop Technique for a Hook/Curl Dropper

The defender should take a 45-degree angle aiming 12 to 14 yards inside the original alignment of the #2, #3, and #4 receivers (Diagram 3-1). Once the drop has begun, he should maintain inside leverage reading the keys and get his head on a "swivel." The routes of the receivers will determine the width and depth of the drop. The coverage will determine how deep to carry a receiver.

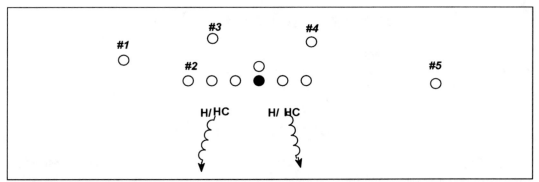

Diagram 3-1. A defender taking a 45-degree angle and aiming 12 to 14 yards inside the original alignment of the #2, #3, and #4 receivers

Head Position on Break of the Receiver and Arm Distance

Head position is the most difficult thing to teach on a receiver's break. When catching up to a receiver, the defender must look to the receiver and not look back to the quarterback until he is an arm distance away from the receiver. How many times have you seen a defender on the receiver's break look to the quarterback and lose three steps? The defender must be disciplined to drive his body and his head to the receiver (Diagram 3-2). He should drive to the receiver's shoulder that is away from the line of scrimmage unless he can get two hands on the ball.

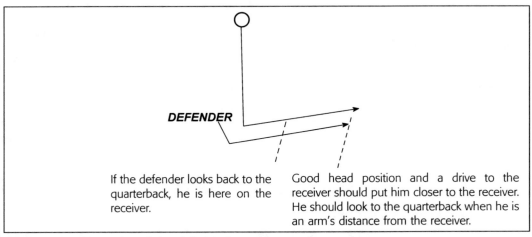

If the defender looks back to the quarterback, he is here on the receiver.

Good head position and a drive to the receiver should put him closer to the receiver. He should look to the quarterback when he is an arm's distance from the receiver.

Diagram 3-2. Examples of the defender's position on the receiver

Leading and Trailing Players

Leading and trailing players (refer to Chapter 2, Diagrams 2-5 and 2-6) give flexibility to any coverage and allow defenders to cover the open receivers. A defender cannot be allowed the excuse of "it isn't my zone" when a receiver is open.

"Cutting" to a Receiver

"Cutting" to a receiver means that when the defender (usually the hook/curl defender) sees a receiver going from the inside to the outside he "cuts" to the inside breaking receiver and turns his back on the quarterback to quickly get into the throwing lane. Once he is in stride with the receiver or an arm distance from the receiver, then he can look back to the quarterback (refer to Chapter 2, Diagrams 2-1 and 2-2). The term "cut" is important in pattern reading (Diagrams 3-3 and 3-4).

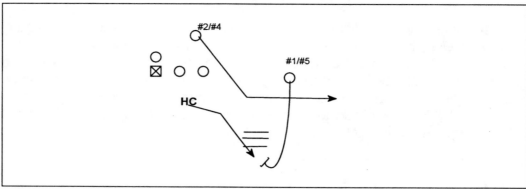

Diagram 3-3. "Cutting" to a receiver (example 1)

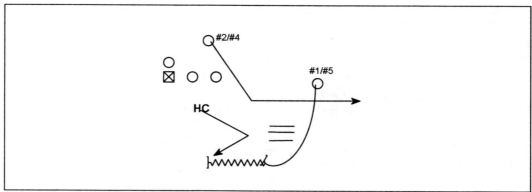

Diagram 3-4. "Cutting" to a receiver (example 2)

Stack and Slide

Stack and slide is used when a defender is stacking off of his key receiver. The defender will stack on his key receiver if this receiver is blocking. The defender now has an opportunity to read the quarterback and slide to any receiver he sees the quarterback looking towards (Diagrams 3-5 and 3-6).

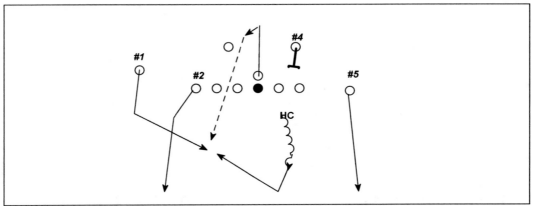

Diagram 3-5. Stack and slide: key receiver blocks and defender reads the quarterback (example 1)

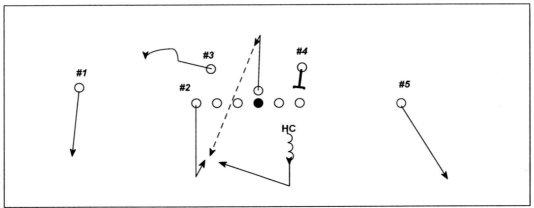

Diagram 3-6. Stack and slide: key receiver blocks and defender reads the quarterback (example 2)

"Push"

A push call is made by an adjacent defender to push the other defender past the coverage towards the next threat (Diagram 3-7).

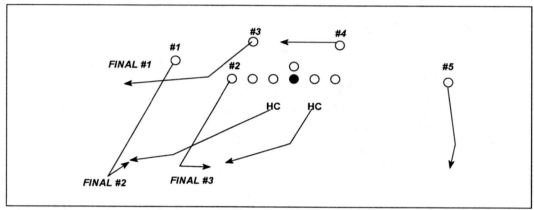

Diagram 3-7. Pushing an adjacent defender to the next threat alerts the frontside hook/curl defender to push through to the final #2 receiver.

"I'm Here"

"I'm here" is simply a call to alert an adjacent defender that the defender making the call is available to help or pick up a coverage (Diagram 3-8).

Note: Although "push" and "I'm here" can be field calls, they can also be used as terms and techniques for pickup patterns in a classroom or on the sideline.

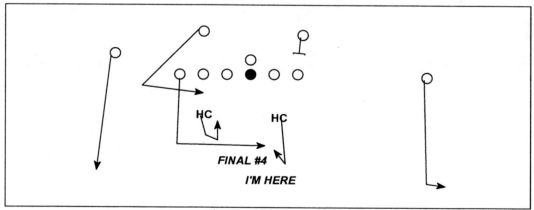

Diagram 3-8. "I'm here" call

Buzz Flat

The flat technique was discussed in Chapter 2; however, "buzzing the flat" is used without pattern reading. The flat defender, based on the coverage, will sprint outside to the widest receiver on a pass play. He will attempt to take away all outside routes. This strategy will usually be coordinated with a specific coverage (e.g., deep third defender playing the inside technique; Diagram 3-9).

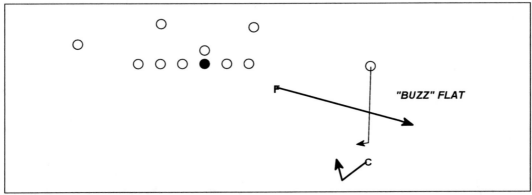

Diagram 3-9. "Buzzing the flat"

Second Through the Zone

Every flat defender must cover the second receiver through the flat by man-to-man coverage. The first receiver should clear out the area, which will force the flat defender to cover the second receiver in the flat (Diagram 3-10).

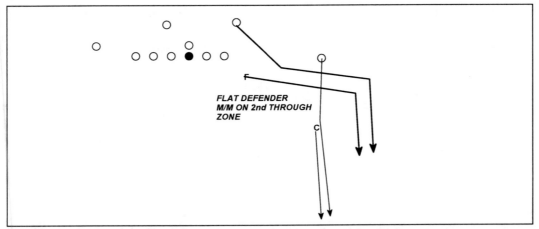

Diagram 3-10. A flat defender covering the second receiver through the zone by man-to-man coverage

Working the Shoulder

Working the shoulder is used when a receiver turns and hooks toward the quarterback to form a wall to block the defender. The defender should "work" to one of the receiver's shoulders to allow him to get his arm between the receiver and the ball (Diagrams 3-11 and 3-12). When working a shoulder, the defender must be tight enough to the shoulder of the receiver to secure the tackle on the receiver if the pass is completed.

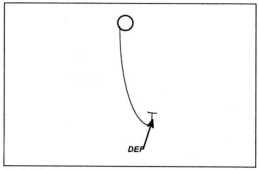

Diagram 3-11. On his approach, the defender is directly behind the receiver. It is tough to make a play on the ball.

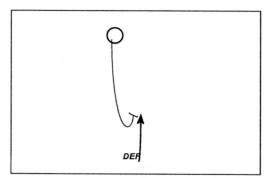

Diagram 3-12. The defender is working to the shoulder of the receiver to knock the ball down.

Eyes and Body

In any zone coverage with pattern reading, a defender, such as a stack defender, will usually have the ability to take away a route with his body and take away another route with his eyes. The defender could also be any player who has achieved position on a receiver and looks back for another receiver (Diagrams 3-13 and 3-14).

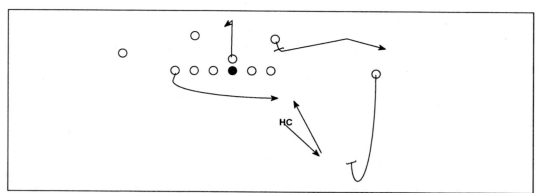

Diagram 3-13. The hook/curl defender has taken away the curl and looked back to the quarterback. His body took away the curl; his eyes will help on the crosser.

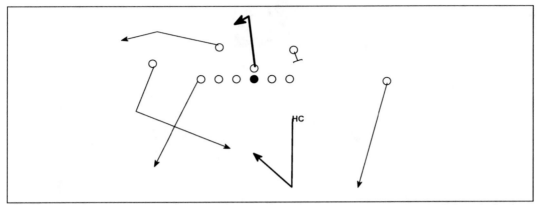

Diagram 3-14. The hook/curl defender's key blocked, and the quarterback is definitely looking away. The hook/curl defender's body took away the curl; he knows his eyes can help underneath.

Once a defender's body is in place to take away a route, his eyes should go to the quarterback or the next receiver in the route progression. Teaching eyes and body to a defender makes him aware in zone drops that it is important to know the next threat and where it could come from based on the pattern being run.

Eyes: Seeing the Key

The keys to read for defenders and the five basic actions that could occur were mentioned in Chapter 2. If a receiver is going outside, a hook/curl defender should be thinking that a receiver is coming inside (from an outside alignment). If a receiver does not come inside, then the defender's thought and his eyes should look for someone coming behind him (Diagram 3-15)—basically, one defender is covering two areas in a zone coverage.

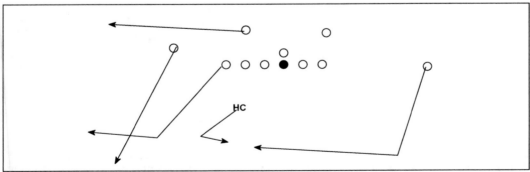

Diagram 3-15. Example of being aware of the route being executed. The defender's eyes tell him the following: if no one to cover, look over my shoulder.

4

Covering Crossers

The biggest, and maybe most difficult, discussion is how to handle crossing receivers. Should a defender pick them up and run with them or pass them off to another defender across the formation? The coverage called will dictate this issue in many cases. It does not matter where the crossing receiver comes from (#1, #2, #3, #4, or #5 receiver); the defender responsible for the crossing receiver must cover him man-to-man within the zone or have the ability to pass him off to another defender based on the coverage called (Diagram 4-1).

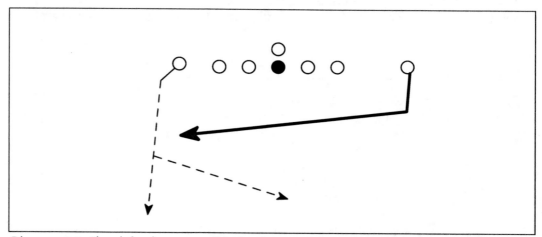

Diagram 4-1. The defender responsible for the crossing receiver must cover him by man-to-man coverage within the zone or have the ability to pass him off to another defender based on the coverage called.

Walling Off

The wall-off technique is used to prevent the crossing receiver from easily crossing the formation (Diagram 4-2). The defender will turn his body to the receiver and form a wall and either force the receiver to go "over the top" of the defender or push off and go back the other way. The critical coaching point for the defender is to step toward the line of scrimmage and then turn to the receiver, with no "daylight" underneath. If the receiver continues across, the defender will turn and run with him after forcing the receiver on top.

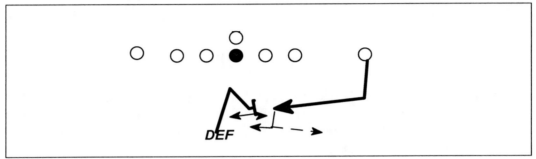

Diagram 4-2. Wall-off technique

Intersecting

Another way to handle the crossing receiver is to allow him to go underneath the defender; the defender will then come "down" to the receiver (Diagram 4-3). This technique usually occurs when the defender has achieved "depth" in his drop. The defender must anticipate where the receiver will be. If the defender comes "down" to the receiver on a straight line, he will be past him (Diagram 4-4).

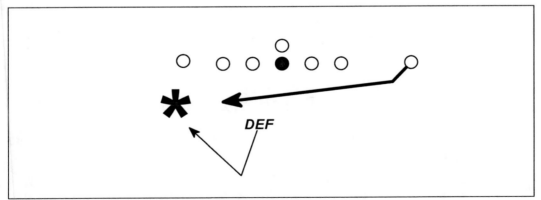

Diagram 4-3. Intersecting the crossing receiver

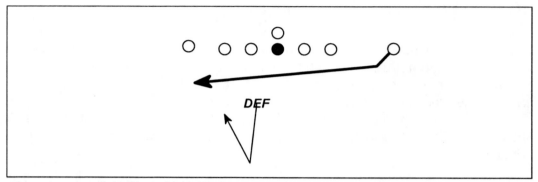

Diagram 4-4. A defender behind the throw

Passing Off

Passing off occurs when a defender is available across the formation based on the pattern being executed (as in the "I'm here" call) (Diagram 4-5). When the defender passes off the low crossing receiver, he must immediately climb to the next level. Someone will be coming in behind him.

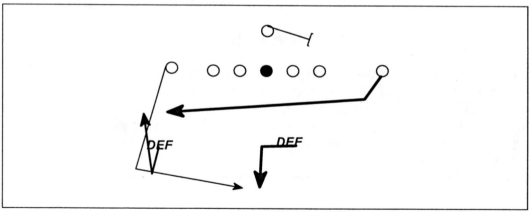

Diagram 4-5. Passing off

Problems

No matter how a crosser is picked up in a zone, a problem will exist. Following are common problems:

- *Walling off*: If a wideout is matched up with a linebacker, then the advantage goes to the wideout. The linebacker forcing the receiver on top at least has a chance to jam him and to turn and run, buying time for the rush to arrive.

- *Intersecting*: This technique is used when the receiver is going across the field uncovered at full speed. Intersecting the receiver is critical because he could outrun the defender.
- *Passing off*: Two things must be realized with passing off. First, the defender away from the crosser must be available. When pattern reading, this strategy is not always assured. Second, the crossing receiver may just hook up to an open area before he reaches the next zone. Passing off a receiver is always the easiest technique to teach but may have the lowest success rate for preventing a completion. Some teams will allow a completion to happen easily based on the route being called.

Finding the #3 Receiver

When picking up patterns, it becomes important to know where the #3 receiver is located and where he goes after the snap. In general, the defender away from the #3 receiver must be alert to cover the receiver in his zone alone (Diagrams 4-6 and 4-7). Refer to Chapters 7 through 9 for more discussion on this technique.

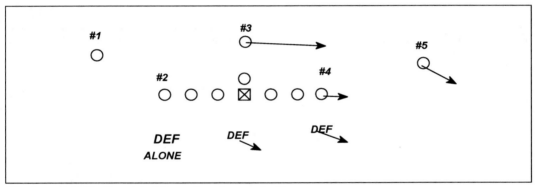

Diagram 4-6. Finding the #3 receiver (example 1)

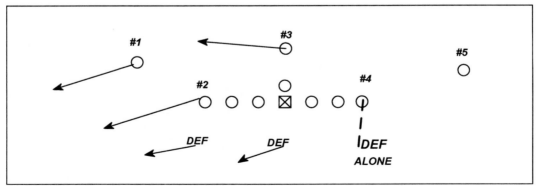

Diagram 4-7. Finding the #3 receiver (example 2)

Low Crosser's Influence on the Defender

When being asked to jam a crosser, the defender must be aware of being a "sucker": the low crossing receiver lets the defender jam him so that a high crosser can come behind the defender. The defender must get a quick jam (not staying with the jam too long) and immediately drive deep to the vacated area behind the defender (Diagram 4-8).

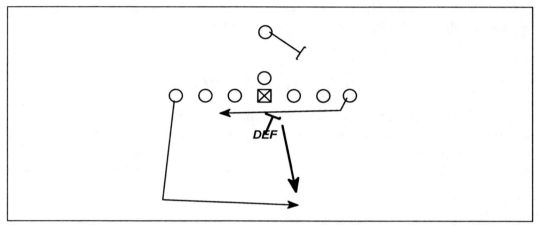

Diagram 4-8. The defender gets a quick jam and immediately climbs to the next level. He must expect a crosser behind him.

5

Covering Seams

It was mentioned previously that seams can hurt a defense in a "big way." If a defense allows defenders to come off seam routes, then too large of a "window" to throw through will exist. One of the purposes of pattern reading is for defenders to stay on seams, with other defenders picking up low crossers. Diagram 5-1 illustrates the typical pattern-read pickup (although it may vary based on the coverage called). By contrast, Diagram 5-2 illustrates the large window that results from a conventional pickup.

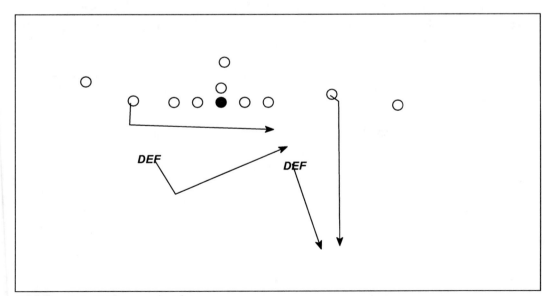

Diagram 5-1. Pattern-read pickup

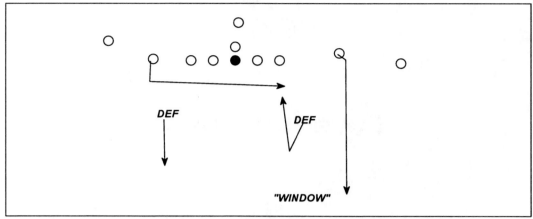

Diagram 5-2. Conventional pickup

Seam Technique

The technique for covering seams is usually determined by the coverage called. However, whether the defender is inside or outside, the technique is relatively the same. The defender carrying the seam must drive hard for the upfield shoulder of the receiver. The position on the receiver depends on where the defender is dropping from in his zone coverage. Usually, he will turn into the receiver. When the receiver extends his arms, the defender must put his hands into the receiver's hands. If the defender is on top of the receiver, he may be able to look back and see the throw. Without a free safety (two deep or zone dog), the defender must maintain the inside position and use any help he has deep (Diagram 5-3). With a middle safety, the seam defender must work to make the transition to the outside shoulder of the receiver to help the free safety, which is not always possible (Diagram 5-4).

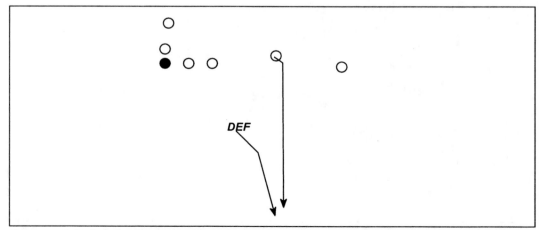

Diagram 5-3. A defender maintaining the inside position and using any help he has deep

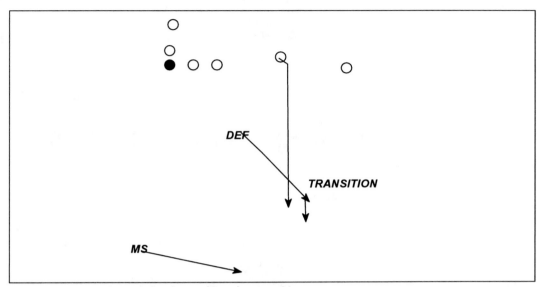

Diagram 5-4. A seam defender making the transition

Flat Defender on the Seam

When a flat defender has no threats, he can help carry a seam or help on a low crosser rather than "cover air." When helping on the seams or other routes, the flat defender cannot turn his back on the quarterback or the formation (Diagram 5-5).

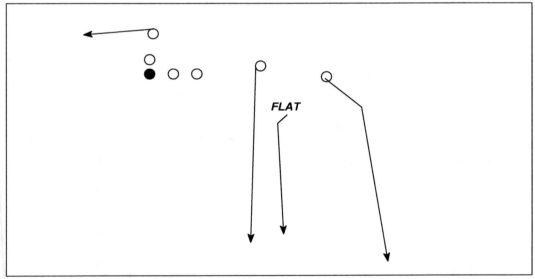

Diagram 5-5. A flat defender can help on the seams, but he must have vision underneath. No threats allow him a deeper cushion.

6

Understanding Pass Concepts

When teaching pattern progression, it is important to understand how an offense is going to attack a defense. No matter what your philosophy might be, you must understand what an offense is trying to do to the defensive scheme. The technique presented in this book describes pattern concepts in words rather than numbers because players seem to get better mental pictures with words. Note: The pass concept diagrams throughout this chapter are intended to highlight only the particular concept being discussed; therefore, full formations are not shown.

High/low (vertical stretch) (Diagram 6-1): The hi/low concept is an attempt to get the defender to attack the low throw to hit the high receiver. Usually, a receiver needs 10 yards of separation (unless he is moving). When the defender is caught in this situation, he must be under the deep receiver with his body; his eyes should look to the quarterback or the short receiver. Reading the quarterback is difficult, since his vision is usually directed to the same line on the receivers. It takes great discipline to cover the high receiver and react to the low receiver.

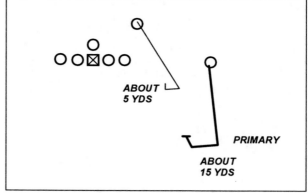

Diagram 6-1. High/low (vertical stretch)

Trail (Diagram 6-2): In the trail route, the second receiver trails the first receiver and breaks off his butt to an open area based on the coverage. The first receiver is trying to clear the area. The coverage will dictate the coaching points, but the trail receiver is looking for an open area. The defender must recover quickly since the receiver is working away from any zone coverage.

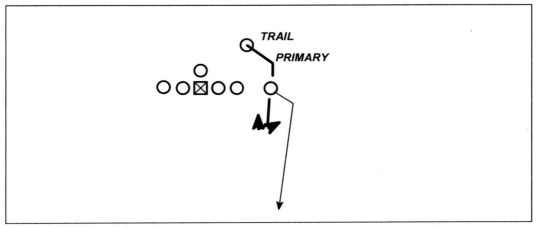

Diagram 6-2. The trail route

Hi/low on the move (Diagram 6-3): The hi/low on the move concept is used to pull the low defender (usually the hook defender) to the short five-yard route while the deeper receiver gets to the vacated area that the defender left. It allows the high receiver to be moving on the catch. The defender must be aware of what is happening and turn to the deep receiver. Hopefully, a flat defender can get close to the low receiver.

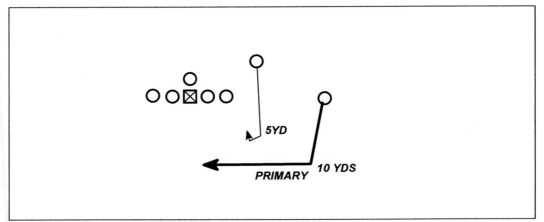

Diagram 6-3. Hi/low on the move

Three out (strong/weak) for the curl (horizontal stretch) (Diagram 6-4): In the three out (strong/weak) for the curl (horizontal stretch) concept, the offense is trying to stretch the defense horizontally to clear the curl for the receiver who slides to an open area at 15 yards usually between the numbers and the hash mark. Defensively, a push call can get a fourth defender to that side. Naturally, the route may vary, but someone usually will be in that curl area.

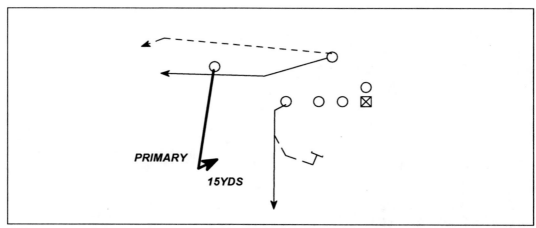

Diagram 6-4. Three out (strong/weak) for the curl (horizontal stretch)

Three out (strong/weak) for the dig (horizontal stretch) (Diagram 6-5): In the three out (strong/weak) for the dig (horizontal stretch), an attempt is made to clear the seam area to allow the receiver to catch the ball on the move (dig). If a defender is pushing to the primary receiver, he may have to turn his back to the quarterback to keep up with the dig receiver.

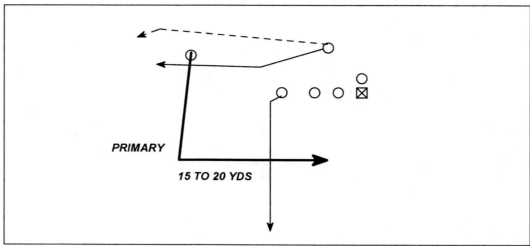

Diagram 6-5. Three out (strong/weak) for the dig (horizontal stretch)

Three out (strong/weak) fan (overload) (Diagram 6-6): In the three out (strong/weak) fan (overload) concept, the offense is overloading the zone on three levels to get the flat defender to jump the low receiver and open the area 15 to 20 yards deep. The flat defender must play deep to short. He should also be aware of the crosser. In this situation, a defender must look back over his shoulder when an inside breaking receiver is not present.

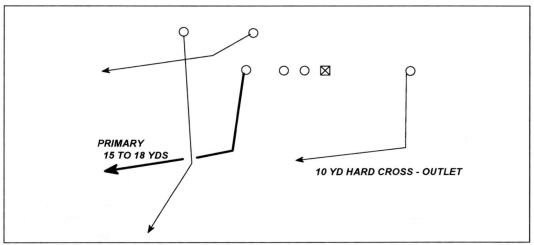

Diagram 6-6. Three out (strong/weak) fan (overload)

Bunch route (clear and option) (Diagram 6-7): The bunch route is designed to clear out for the outside receiver to run a short 5- to 10-yard option route inside. It is sometimes run with a flow (four receivers to a side), which makes the route easier to cover since the defense can immediately push an extra defender. In this situation, any hook/curl defender must jump the option quickly. The flat receiver is usually the outlet. The corner route is usually thrown on a defensive breakdown (refer to Chapter 2, Diagrams 2-5 and 2-6).

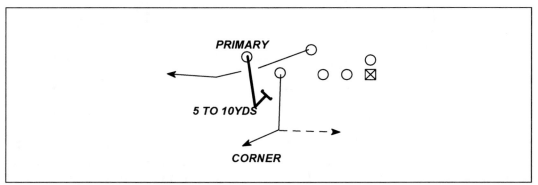

Diagram 6-7. Bunch route (clear and option)

All-in (favored out of trips with hi/low concept) (Diagram 6-8): The all-in route is a concept used to get the ball to the final #2 or #3 receiver who is on the move. The outside receiver is usually the outlet. This route pickup will apply the leading/trailing concept (refer to Chapter 2, Diagrams 2-5 and 2-6).

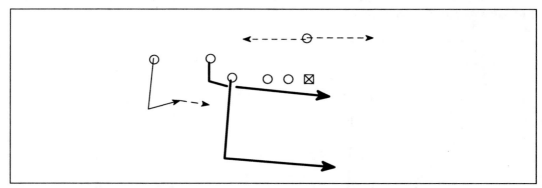

Diagram 6-8. All-in (favored out of trips with hi/low concept)

Clear and cross route (Diagram 6-9): In the clear and cross route, the low crosser is primary. The offside will clear out that side with seams or out and up, attempting to isolate the inside defender to the low crosser. The low crosser will do whatever is necessary to get open. If faced with a wall-off technique (refer to Chapter 4, Diagram 4-2), he may work back to the side from where he came, which is why the #3 receiver will not checkdown inside. The clear and cross route is favored by offenses from the +15-yard line in to the goal line.

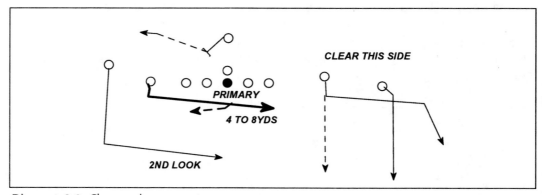

Diagram 6-9. Clear and cross route

Cross and dig route (Diagram 6-10): The cross and dig route is the same as the clear and cross route except that the low crosser from the other side will control the underneath coverage. The inside defender who is working the seam must be aware of the deep inside break by the outside receiver.

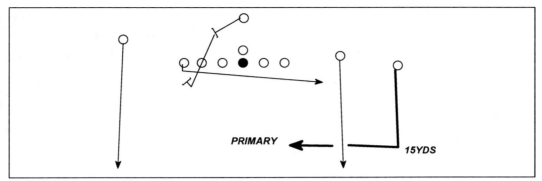

Diagram 6-10. Cross and dig route

Seams (Diagram 6-11): Seams were discussed in Chapter 5. Usually, the inside #2 and #4 receivers are primary based on the coverage called. Obviously, they will throw away from the single safety.

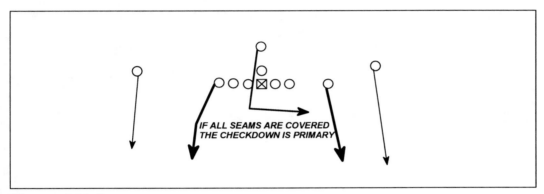

Diagram 6-11. Seams

Trips seams (Diagram 6-12): Trips seams are mostly designed to get a throwing lane for the #2 receiver.

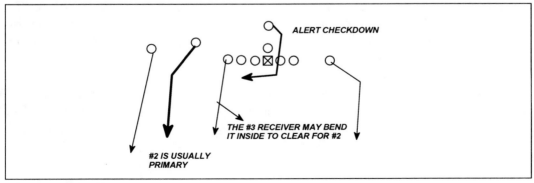

Diagram 6-12. Trips seams

Scissors (Diagram 6-13): In the scissors concept, the corner route is usually primary. This concept is used to create a dilemma for the deep-coverage defenders (half-coverage or deep-outside third defenders). The flat receiver is strictly an outlet receiver.

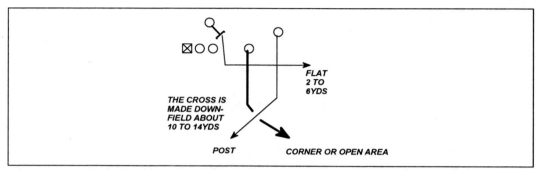

Diagram 6-13. Scissors

All option (Diagram 6-14): In the all-option concept, depth is anywhere from 5 to 10 yards. It is a "get open" route away from the technique of the defender. The receivers are split far enough so that the defenders are isolated in the zone coverage.

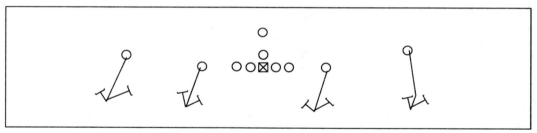

Diagram 6-14. All option

Smash/option (Diagram 6-15): The smash/option concept is used more than 5 under 2 deep coverage. If the curl/seam defender leaves the inside receiver to soon, then the receiver will hook up to any open area. The defender's eyes should be on the outside (#1 or #5) receiver, but his body should be taking away the inside route. When the outside receiver stops his route, then the inside defender will stop his drop into coverage and hold off the inside receiver.

Smash/corner (Diagram 6-16): The smash/corner concept is also used versus 5 under 2 deep coverages. The inside defender should stop his drop when the outside receiver stops. Once the inside receiver goes to the corner, the inside defender (seam/curl) should drive to the outside (#1 or #5) receiver.

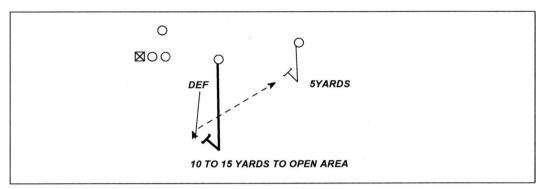

Diagram 6-15. Smash/option

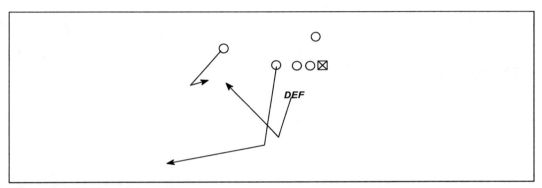

Diagram 6-16. Smash/corner

Outs (Diagram 6-17): The outs route is designed to get the ball to the inside receiver. The outside receiver releases out to assure a "window" is open for the quarterback.

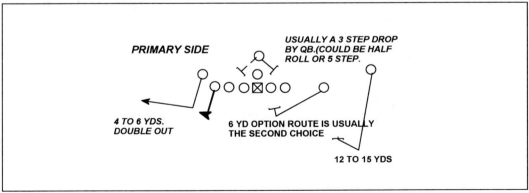

Diagram 6-17. Outs

(Double) slants (Diagram 6-18): In the (double) slants concept, the #1 and #2 receivers will have a substantial split between them. If the #2 receiver is covered, then #1 receiver is primary.

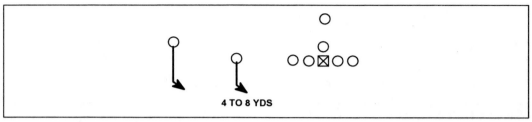

Diagram 6-18. (Double) slants

Out/slant (Diagram 6-19): In the out/slant concept, the outside breaking receiver is trying to open the throwing alley for the slant. The quarterback will execute a three-step drop. This concept is frequently used versus the blitz.

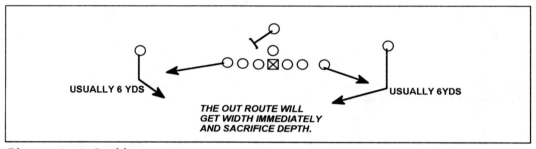

Diagram 6-19. Out/slant

Double cross (Diagram 6-20): In the double-cross concept, three levels of crossers may be used. This route is designed to clear an area for the high crossers.

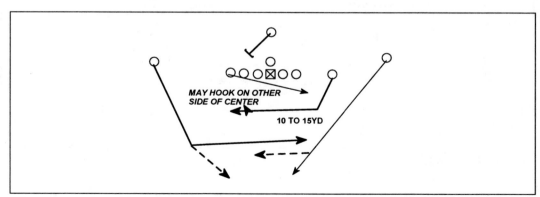

Diagram 6-20. Double cross

All hook/option (Diagram 6-21): In the double-cross concept, the strongside is all option/hooks designed to open the area for #2 and #3. Note that the flat is controlled by a receiver aligned there or by a back to the flat.

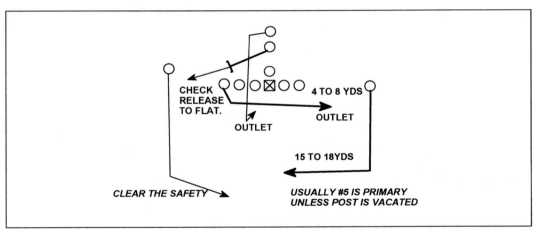

Diagram 6-21. All hook/option

Flow pass (NCAA) (Diagram 6-22): The flow pass is an age-old route that is still highly successful as a result of the play-action that creates a hole in the square-in area. One of the hook/curl defenders must turn and run to the square-in area.

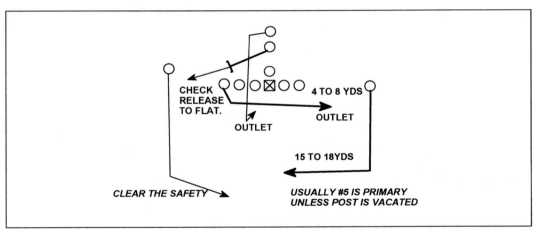

Diagram 6-22. Flow pass (NCAA)

Cover 4 beater (Diagram 6-23): The cover 4 beater route is mostly used versus quarter coverage when the safety is squatting on the #2 or #4 receiver. The corner is basically one-on-one with the widest receiver. The safety is in a "bind." The burden is on the outside defender.

Bootleg concept (Diagram 6-24): In the bootleg route, the crosser must be taken by a hook/curl defender who must get to an "intersection" point by turning and running with the crossing tight end. The flat receiver is the first threat to the defense.

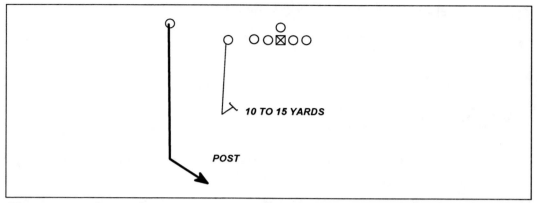

Diagram 6-23. Cover 4 beater

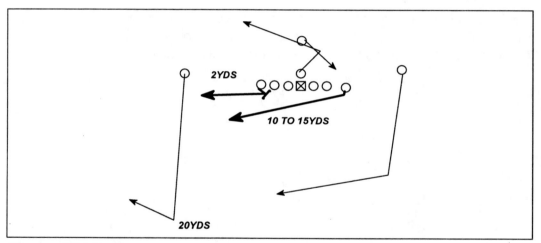

Diagram 6-24. Bootleg concept

Importance of Knowing Pass Concepts

Understanding pass concepts is an important step in teaching the coverages used in pass defense. Knowing what an offense is trying to do to a defense is just as important as teaching the coverages. It is impossible to cover all patterns, but concepts stay the same. The personnel, the side, or one route may change. When preparing for a specific opponent, the concepts are more important than the patterns. Usually, the routes will change, but the primary concepts seldom change for a given team.

7

Coverages in 4 Under 3 Deep

For zone coverages, 4 under 3 deep, 5 under 2 deep, 3 under 4 across, and combination zones will be discussed. With a four-man rush, these zones are the most used coverages. The positions in the coverages rather than who is in the positions (e.g., safety or linebacker) will be discussed. The technique and the responsibilities of the positions are most important.

4 Under 3 Deep (Base Pattern)

In 4 under 3 deep coverage, the four short zones (two flats and two hook/curls) are covered by linebackers and/or safeties or nickel or dime defenses (Diagram 7-1).

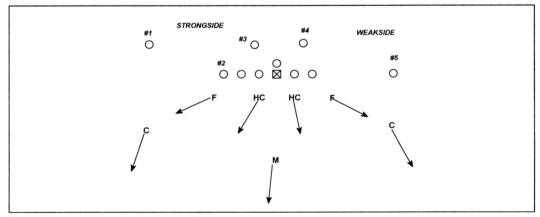

Diagram 7-1. 4 under 3 deep coverage.

Flat defender (F): Usually is a linebacker and/or safety or a nickel and dime defender. Covers any outside releasing receivers. The preliminary drop is inside the original alignment for the #1 or #5 receiver. Maintains outside leverage on the #2, #3, and #4 receivers; must be as wide as the widest #2, #3, or #4 receiver. Never turns his back on the quarterback.

Hook/curl defender (HC): Covers any inside breaking receiver. The aiming points are 5 to 15 yards deep inside the #2, #3, and #4 receivers. Must be alert to carry seams.

Outside deep-third defenders (C): Covers the deepest receiver in the outside one-third of the field. If no deep threat exists, covers the outside receiver man-to-man after 12 yards.

Deep-third middle defender (M): Checks seams.

The rest of this chapter provides several examples of 4 under 3 deep patterns to show how the route pickups occur and how each position's rule would be applied.

Pattern #1

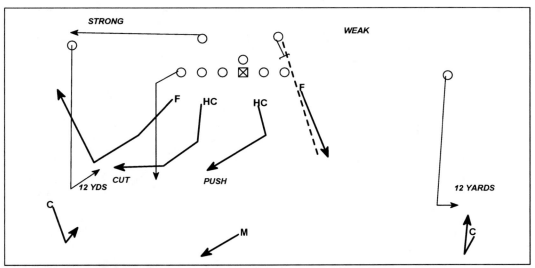

Diagram 7-2. Pattern #1

Strongside F: Cushions through the curl; when the flat receiver crosses his face, he works to the flat.

Strongside HC: Works to the final #3 receiver (seam); on a push call, goes to the final #2 (curl) receiver and cuts to him.

Weakside HC: Watches the #4 receiver; if he delays at all, the weakside HC gets to the final #3 receiver and makes a push call to the strongside HC.

Weakside F: Starts drop under the #5 receiver, but watches the #4 receiver; after the cushion, plays the #4 receiver man-to-man on the checkdown with depth.

C (strong): Defends deep one-third and maintains depth on the #1 and #2 receivers; if no threat exists, closes on the curl.

C (weak): Defends deep one-third, but with no threat, covers the #5 receiver man-to-man; does not cover air.

M: Middle deep one-third; must be alert for a receiver down the seam.

Pattern #2

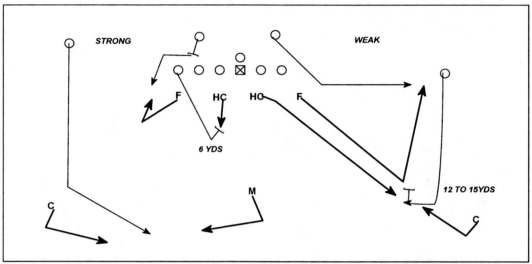

Diagram 7-3. Pattern #2

Weakside F: Cushions through the curl; when the flat receiver crosses his face, he works to the flat.

Weakside HC: Cuts to the curl by the #5 receiver.

Strongside HC: Inside position on the #2 and/or the #3 receiver (the final #3 receiver is shown in the diagram).

Strongside F: Starts drop to the #1 receiver; with no flat threat, works to the next threat (back), remembering outside leverage on the #2, #3, and #4 receivers.

C (strong): Defends the deep one-third and outside leverage on the post "squeeze."

C (weak): Defends the deep one-third; with no threat deep, closes on the curl.

M: Middle deep one-third; clears the seams, and then gets to the post.

Pattern #3

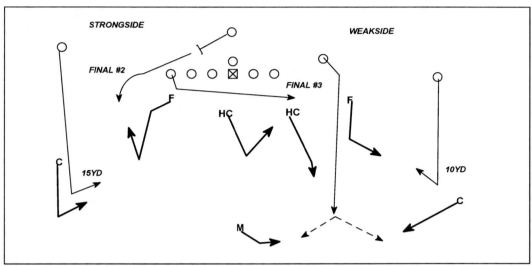

Diagram 7-4. Pattern #3

Strongside F: Drops under the #1 receiver; maintains outside leverage on the #2 and #3 receivers.

Strongside HC: Covers the final #3 receiver.

Weakside HC: Opens inside to the #4 receiver (the rule is inside the #3 or #4 receiver; the #3 receiver is gone). Carries the seam unless the #5 receiver is on the short route; when in doubt, he carries the seam.

Weakside F: Outside position on the #4 receiver; tries to jam him inside, and works inside the #5 receiver.

Strongside C: No threat to the outside one-third; closes on the curl.

Weakside C: Covers the deepest threat to the one-third from the outside in (the #4 receiver).

M: Most dangerous to the post (the #4 receiver).

Pattern #4

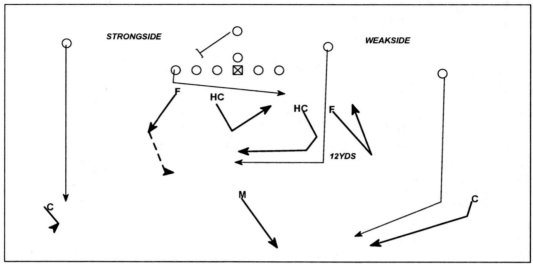

Diagram 7-5. Pattern #4

Strongside F: Starts to the #1 receiver, and maintains outside leverage on the #2 and #3 receivers (back); looks for crossers, and does not cover air.

Strongside HC: Inside the final #3 receiver (pass off may be discussed)

Weakside HC: Takes away the #4 receiver on the square-in route; he may have to turn his back to keep up, thereby switching to man-to-man coverage.

Weakside H: Gets under the #1 receiver and hunts for crossers.

Strongside C: Covers the #1 receiver.

Weakside C: Squeezes the post.

M: Post.

Pattern #5

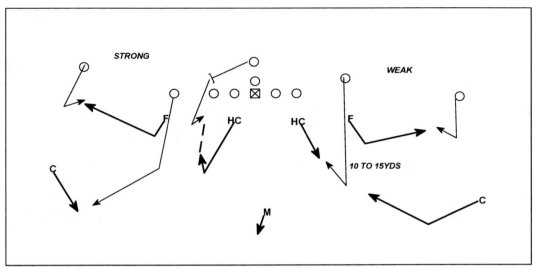

Diagram 7-6. Pattern #5

Strongside F: Drives to the #1 receiver who is in the flat.

Strongside HC: When the #2 receiver disappears, closes hard on the #3 receiver.

Weakside HC: Inside the #4 receiver.

Weakside F: Drives to the #5 receiver.

Strongside C: Deepest of the #1 and #2 receivers.

Weakside C: If no threat, then closes to the ball.

M: Breaks on the ball; reads the quarterback.

Pattern #6

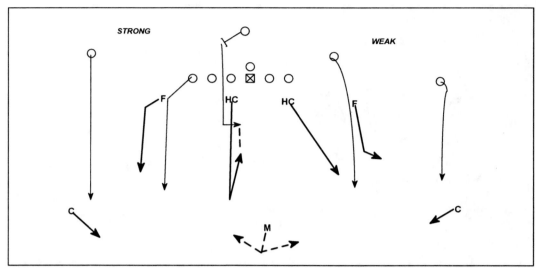

Diagram 7-7. Pattern #6

Strongside F: If no threat to the flat, holds off outside portion of the seam.

Strongside HC: Drops inside the #2 receiver and outside the #3 receiver; if no flat threat, then comes off the #2 receiver and closes on the #3 receiver.

Weakside HC: Inside the #4 receiver; carries the seam.

Weakside F: Outside portion of the #4 receiver.

Strongside C: Deepest of the #1 and #2 receivers; runs inside the #1 receiver and outside the #2 receiver. Watches the quarterback and the ball thrown.

Weakside C: Deepest of the #4 and #5 receivers; runs inside the #5 receiver and outside the #4 receiver. Watches the quarterback and the ball thrown.

M: Maintains deep leverage on the #2 and #4 receivers; watches the quarterback and the ball.

Pattern #7

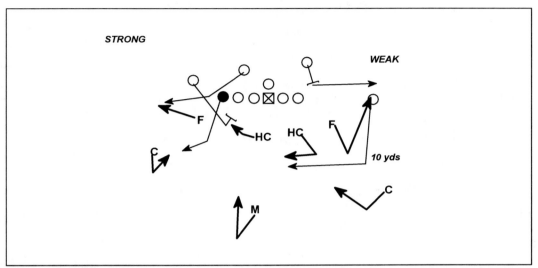

Diagram 7-8. Pattern #7

Strongside F: Covers the flat.

Strongside HC: Covers the first inside breaker (wall-off technique).

Weakside HC: Covers the inside breaker (the final #4 receiver); turns with him man-to-man.

Weakside F: Inside the #5 receiver, breaks to the flat receiver.

Strongside C: Covers the deep threat.

Weakside C: If no threat, closes on the most dangerous receiver.

M: Reads the quarterback, and breaks on the throw.

Pattern #8 (Flow)

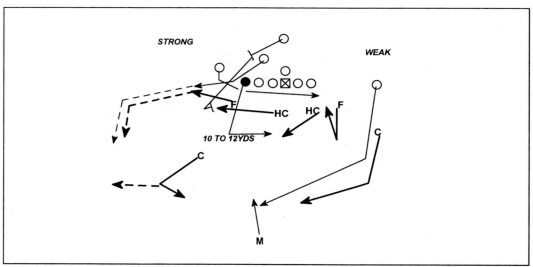

Diagram 7-9. Pattern #8 (flow)

Strongside F: Covers the flat receiver man-to-man.

Strongside HC: Has two defenders behind him (because the play is "flow"); covers the final #2 receiver.

Weakside HC: Flow tells him that he has one defender behind him; covers the next inside breaker.

Weakside F: Watches the first crosser and covers man-to-man.

Strongside C: Does not cover air; hunts for crossers or flat receivers breaking deep.

Weakside C: Squeezes the post.

M: Post.

Pattern #9 (Flow)

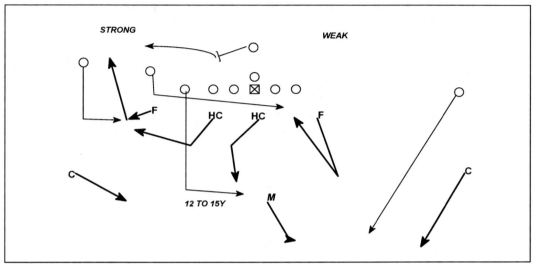

Diagram 7-10. Pattern #9 (flow)

Strongside F: Stacks and slides with the #1 receiver until the final #1 receiver crosses his face (the back).

Strongside HC: If flow, lets two receivers go and gets to the final #2 receiver.

Weakside HC: If flow, lets one receiver go and gets to the next level; covers man-to-man.

Weakside F: If flow, takes the first crosser; works high to low.

Strongside C: Closes to the middle; checks deep crossers to the square.

Weakside C: Closes on the post.

M: Post.

Pattern #10

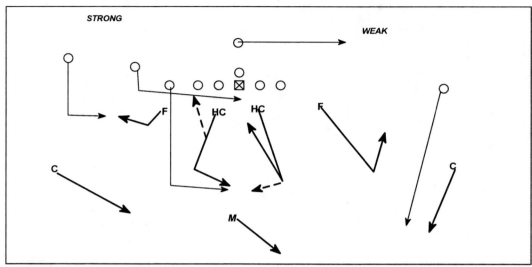

Diagram 7-11. Pattern #10

Strongside F: The only flat threat is the #1 receiver.

Strongside HC: Covers the #2 or #3 receiver. He cannot be wrong because the weakside HC must play off him; leading/trailing player (refer to Chapter 2, Diagrams 2-5 and 2-6).

Weakside HC: Plays off the strongside HC, and covers the open receiver of the inside breakers; leading/trailing player (refer to Chapter 2, Diagrams 2-5 and 2-6).

Weakside F: Is under the #5 receiver to the flat (flare).

Strongside C: Drives to the post.

Weakside C: Covers the #5 receiver man-to-man.

M: Deep threat to the middle of the field.

Pattern #11

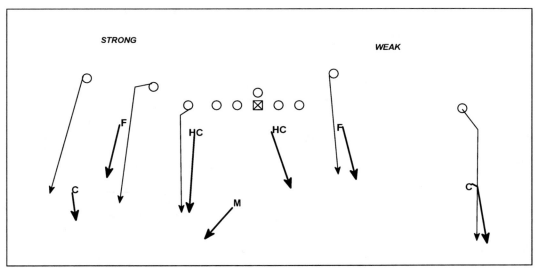

Diagram 7-12. Pattern #11

Strongside F: If no flat threat, holds the outside portion of the seam on the #2 receiver.

Strongside HC: The #3 receiver is down the seam (refer to Chapter 5).

Weakside HC: Covers the inside portion of the #4 receiver; must be alert to come off on any inside breaking receiver.

Weakside F: If no flat threat, holds the outside portion of the seam on the #4 receiver.

Strongside C: Gets between the #1 receiver and the #2 receiver; reads the quarterback to the ball.

Weakside C: Covers the #5 receiver.

M: Covers the middle one-third, and reads the quarterback to the ball; must be alert to the trips side.

Pattern #12 (Flow)

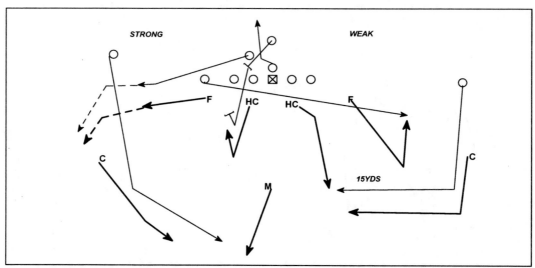

Diagram 7-13. Pattern #12 (flow)

Strongside F: Covers the flat receiver; must be alert to the second receiver through the zone.

Strongside HC: Must be alert for a checkdown.

Weakside HC: Passes the first crosser to the F since the F is available, and then drives (cuts) to the inside breaker to either side (the #5 receiver is shown in the diagram); the #1 receiver could be running the square-in route, and the #5 receiver could be running the post.

Weakside F: Is under the #5 receiver; covers the next threat to the flat (the low crosser), and covers the first open crosser.

Strongside C: Covers the post from the outside in.

Weakside C: Covers the square-in route from over the top; possibly drives to the post and replaces the M.

M: Covers the post. (*Note*: It is possible to drive to the square-in route and let the corner drive to the post; be aware that the pattern must express itself quickly, and it can be risky.)

8

Coverages in 5 Under 2 Deep

As previously mentioned, the positions in the coverages rather than who is in the positions (e.g., safety or linebacker) will be discussed. The technique and the responsibilities of the positions are most important.

5 Under 2 Deep (Base Pattern)

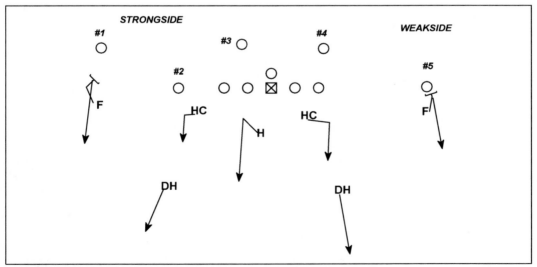

Diagram 8-1. 5 under 2 deep coverage.

Strongside/weakside flat defenders (F): Is a corner. Jams #1 and #5 receivers inside and then cushions back and plays all routes high to low, being as wide as the widest receiver.

Strongside hook/curl/seam defender (H/C): Covers the #2 receiver. Forces the #2 receiver outside. H/C's body maintains inside leverage on the #2 receiver, but his eyes go to the #1 receiver. Carries the seam by the #2 receiver until the #1 receiver stops his route, and then the H/C stops his drop, maintaining inside leverage. If the key (#2) receiver releases outside, cuts to the #1 receiver or any inside breaking receiver.

Weakside hook/curl/seam defender (H/C): Covers the #4 receiver. Forces the #4 receiver outside. H/C's body maintains inside leverage on the #4 receiver, but his eyes go to the #5 receiver. Carries the seam by the #4 receiver until the #5 receiver stops his route, and then the H/C stops his drop, maintaining inside leverage. If the key (#4) receiver releases outside, cuts to the #5 receiver or any inside breaking receiver.

Hook defender (H): Covers the #3 receiver. Must be alert to crossers becoming the #3 receiver. Uses the middle hook (not the Tampa 2 technique).

Strongside/weakside deep-half defender (DH): Maintains one-half coverage of the field, keys outside receivers to the inside receivers, and stays on top of all routes. Maintains inside leverage on the #1 or #5 receiver.

Pattern #1

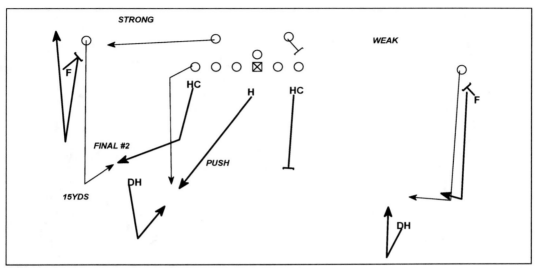

Diagram 8-2. Pattern #1

Strongside F: Cushions and reacts to throw of the flare to the back.

Strongside HC: Pushes through and cuts to the curl for the final #2 receiver.

H: Covers the final #3 receiver, and carries the seam with inside leverage.

Weakside HC: Stacks on the #4 receiver (the key, who blocks); reads the quarterback and slides to the nearest threat.

Weakside F: Cushions; if no flat threat, closes on the #5 receiver.

Strong DH: Covers the seam by the #2 receiver with outside leverage.

Weak DH: Deepest threat is the square-in route (the #5 receiver); jumps the #5 receiver when his shoulders turn inside.

Pattern #2

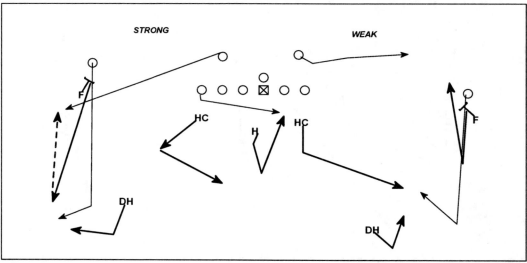

Diagram 8-3. Pattern #2

Strongside F: Cushions and stays under the #1 receiver; breaks on the flat receiver on the throw.

Strongside HC: Starts the cut based on the outside release (the back final #2 receiver); when no receiver is present, he will turn back to the formation to find a receiver.

H: Covers the crosser man-to-man (the final #3 receiver).

Weakside HC: If the key (#4) receiver goes outside, cuts to the #5 receiver.

Weakside F: Cushions to react to the flare by the back.

Strongside DH: Closes on the corner route by the #1 receiver from the inside out.

Weakside DH: If no threat, reads the quarterback, and closes on the curl.

Pattern #3

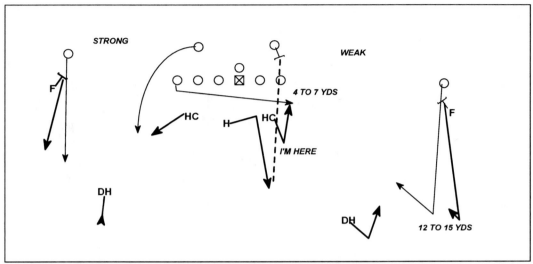

Diagram 8-4. Pattern #3 (refer to Chapter 3, Diagram 3-8, for a description of the "I'm here" call)

Strongside F: Cushions back getting depth.

Strongside HC: Inside the final #2 receiver, carries the seam (the back).

H: Starts coverage, and then drops off and stacks on the final #3 receiver (the back) after the "I'm here" call by the weakside HC (which really needs no call because it is not hard to see).

Weakside HC: Stacks on the #4 receiver, and covers the final #4 receiver (the crosser).

Weakside F: Cushions the back.

Strongside DH: Inside leverage on the #1 receiver, and outside leverage on the final #2 receiver.

Weakside DH: If no threats, closes on the #5 receiver.

Pattern #4

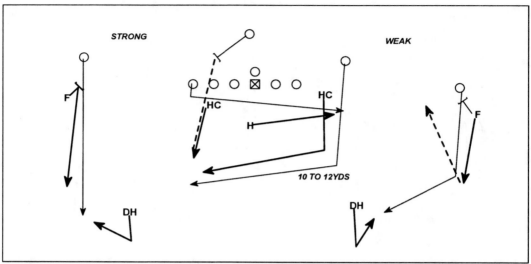

Diagram 8-5. Pattern #4

Strongside F: Cushions; if no threats, maintains cushion.

Strongside HC: Has the #2 receiver on the quick shallow cross, but H is available, so the strongside HC passes the #2 receiver off to H and stacks on the back. He may also help on the crosser (the #3 receiver).

H: The final #3 receiver is the crosser; covers him man-to-man.

Weakside HC: If the #4 receiver drives upfield, covers him, and turns with him to keep in stride.

Weakside F: Cushions, but must be alert for the crosser extending the route; His eyes should be inside to watch the route.

Strongside DH: Maintains inside leverage on the deep receiver.

Weakside DH: Takes away the post from on top and inside.

Pattern #5

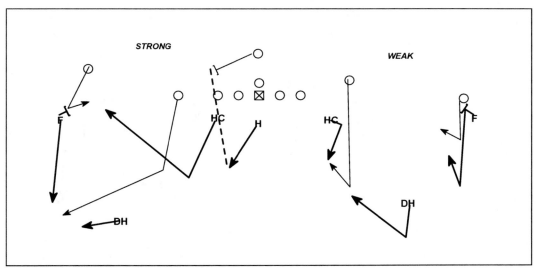

Diagram 8-6. Pattern #5

Strongside F: If the #1 receiver stops his route, cushions the corner route; only the ball should bring the strongside F up to the #1 receiver.

Strongside HC: His body takes away the #2 receiver's seam, but his eyes are on the #1 receiver; when the #1 receiver stops his route, the strongside HC stops the drop, and when the #2 receiver goes outside, the strongside HC drives to the #1 receiver. Drives immediately (does not wait for the throw); does not lose the inside leverage.

H: Stacks on the #3 receiver; if no release by the #3 receiver, reads the quarterback, and hunts the receiver he looks toward.

Weakside HC: His body position inside the #4 receiver; his eyes are on the #5 receiver. When the #5 receiver stops, the weakside HC stops; does not go directly to the #5 receiver. Must hold off the option by the #4 receiver.

Weakside F: Cushions; if no threat, reacts to the #5 receiver short.

Strongside DH: Gets to the corner by the #2 receiver with inside out leverage.

Weakside DH: If no deep receiver, goes to the option.

Pattern #6

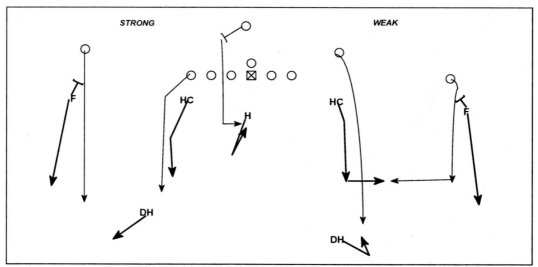

Diagram 8-7. Patten #6

Strongside F: Cushions after the jam.

Strongside HC: Carries the #2 receiver in the seam, and watches the #1 receiver; if he stops the route, then the strongside HC stops and looks for the inside break.

H: Covers the #3 receiver; if no threats, covers him man-to-man.

Weakside HC: Carries the #4 receiver down the seam, and watches the #5 receiver; if he stops, the weakside HC stops; takes away the inside break (which is not easy, especially if the #4 receiver is driving hard downfield, higher than the #5 receiver).

Weakside F: Cushions after the jam; must be alert to the corner by the #4 receiver.

Strongside DH: Gets depth, and plays between the #1 receiver and the #2 receiver if both are going deep; looks for the ball.

Weakside DH: Must be sure to watch the #5 receiver; when he stops, the weakside DH attempts to get back the leverage inside on the #4 receiver.

Pattern #7

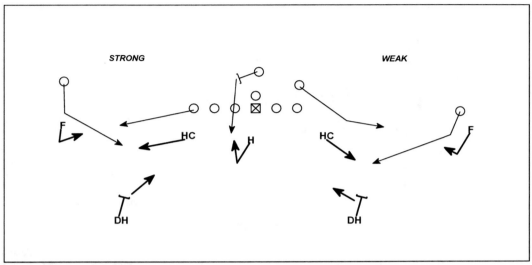

Diagram 8-8. Pattern #7

Strongside F: If no deep threat, attacks the flat receiver; must be alert for a break downfield (second through the zone).

Strongside HC: Cuts to the #1 receiver coming inside.

H: Stacks on the #3 receiver (the back); must be alert to the checkdown by the #3 receiver or the slant getting past the cutters.

Weakside HC: Cuts to the #5 receiver cutting inside.

Weakside F: If no deep threat, attacks the flat receiver; must be alert for a break downfield (second through the zone).

Strongside DH: If no deep threat, must be alert for the slant getting past the cutters.

Weakside DH: If no deep threat, must be alert for the slant getting past the cutters.

Pattern #8

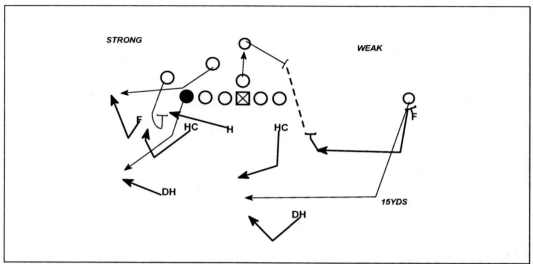

Diagram 8-9. Pattern #8

Strongside F: Cushions deep to the flat but must not allow the widest receiver to cross his face; gets as wide as the widest. (Note: It would be difficult to ask the F to cushion the corner route when the receiver is crossing his face and outflanking him.)

Strongside HC: Drives to the #2 receiver (the tight end); when he breaks to the corner, the strongside HC cushions him or gets to the outside portion of the option route by the final #3 receiver.

H: Drives hard to the final #3 receiver (option).

Weakside HC: Stacks on the key (#4) receiver; when the square-in route comes inside, he becomes the #4 receiver. F will cover him.

Weakside F: Must be wide as the widest receiver; when sliding inside, stops at the new #5 receiver (the back).

Strongside DH: Covers the corner route; may be one-on-one.

Weakside DH: Comes down on the square-in route when no deep threat exists. (*Note*: This pickup is natural; players would probably do it without any coaching.)

Pattern #9

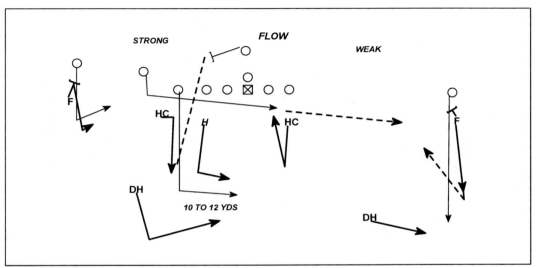

Diagram 8-10. Pattern #9

Strongside F: Cushions; if no threat, closes on the #1 receiver. Does not pass the widest receiver.

Strongside HC: Gets to the final #2 receiver (which is the back, as a result of the flow with the all-in route). Starts high.

H: Passes one receiver back with the flow; lets the first crosser work to the high square-in route.

Weakside HC: Pick up the first crosser (#4 receiver); the flat defender is removed from the formation.

Weakside F: Cushion; be alert to come down on the crosser if he gets away from the weakside HC.

Strongside DH: If no deep threat, closes from on top of the square-in route.

Weakside DH: Works to the #5 receiver.

Pattern #10

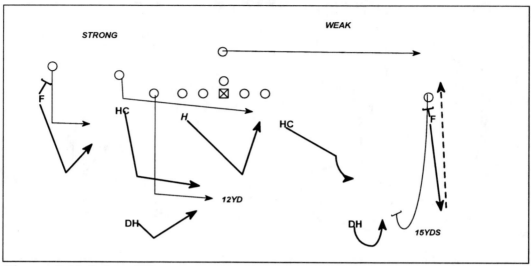

Diagram 8-11. Pattern #10

Basic rule: If backside of trips set, weakside HC should be slow to cut to the #5 receiver; help may be needed on the hard crossers.

Strongside F: Cushions; if no deep threat, closes on the #1 receiver.

Strongside HC: Closes to the final #2 receiver (which is difficult; in the technique, he always goes high when the #2 receiver goes across hard, creating a new final #2 receiver).

H: Not flow; the final #3 is the first crosser. May use wall-off technique.

Weakside HC: If outside release by the #4 receiver, gets under the #5 (final #4) receiver. Should be late to cut, just stack early; may need to help on any open crosser.

Weakside F: Cushions; reacts to throw.

Strongside DH: If no deep threat, closes on the high square-in route.

Weakside DH: If no deep threat, closes on the curl.

Pattern #11

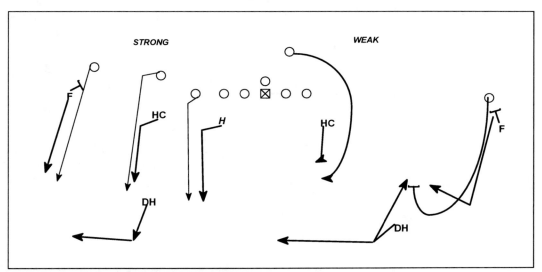

Diagram 8-12. Pattern #11

Strongside F: Cushions; stays deep with no threat underneath.

Strongside HC: Carries the seam (technique described in assignment list for Diagram 8-7).

H: Carries the #3 receiver down the seam (refer to Chapter 6).

Weakside HC: Maintains inside leverage on the #4 receiver.

Weakside F: If no flat threat, closes on the #5 receiver. (Note: If the weakside DH is pushed to the trips side in the game plan, the weakside F should stay on top of the #5 receiver.)

Strongside DH: Gets deep, and reads the quarterback from deep; split receivers based on the hash mark and sideline.

Weakside DH: If no deep threat, closes on the curl. (Note: In preparation, it is possible to push the weakside DH to the trips side.)

Pattern #12 (Flow)

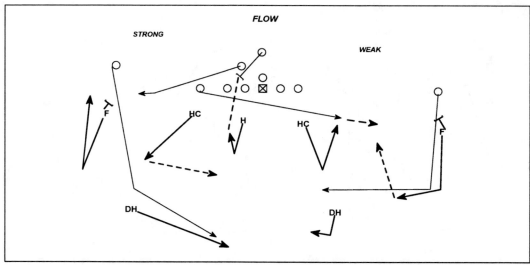

Diagram 8-13. Pattern #12(flow)

Strongside F: Cushions; reacts to the flat.

Strongside HC: Cuts to the #1 receiver; if post by the #1 receiver, turns to formation, and must be alert to the next threat.

H: Stacks on the final #3 receiver; with flow, passes off first crosser.

Weakside HC: Stacks high, and must be alert to the crosser with flow; comes down on the crosser (the final #4 receiver). Weakside F is too far removed to be a factor early.

Weakside F: Cushions and works to the square-in route, but does not pass the low crosser.

Strongside DH: Maintains inside leverage to the post.

Weakside DH: Works on top of the square-in route; must be alert to help on the post.

9

Coverages in 3 Under 4 Across— Quarters

As in previous chapters, the positions in the coverages rather than who is in the positions (e.g., safety or linebacker) will be discussed. The technique and the responsibilities of the positions are important.

3 Under 4 Across—Quarters (Base Pattern)

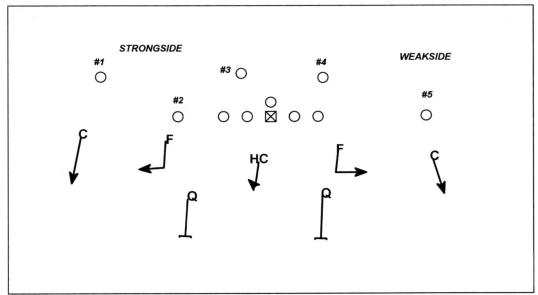

Diagram 9-1. 3 under 4 across—quarters coverage

Flat defender (F): A receiver must bring the F to the flat. The F basically covers the outside portions of the #2, #3, and #4 receivers but from an inside alignment. The initial aiming points should be outside the #2 and #4 receivers from an inside alignment. If the #1 or #5 receiver runs a smash route (short route), goes to it. The reason for the inside alignment is to secure the inside release by the #2 or #4 receiver if the #3 receiver goes away or the #2 and #4 receivers run shallow crossing routes (see Diagram 9-4).

Hook/curl defender (HC): Covers the #3 receiver similar to the 5 under 2 deep technique.

Short- to deep-cover defenders (Q): Basically covers deep- to short-quarter coverage and the #2, #3, and #4 receivers. Covers any seams by the #2, #3, and #4 receivers man-to-man. If the #2, #3, and #4 receivers are on short routes, doubles on the #1 receiver. Covers any route of +12 yards downfield by the #2 or #4 receivers man-to-man.

Deep-third defender (C): Is responsible for the deep-outside quarter, keying the #1 or #5 receiver. At times, this coverage will be man-to-man. Must maintain inside leverage on the #1 and #5 receivers. No guarantee of help inside exists. The reason for the inside technique is to take away the post route since no help is a good possibility. In essence, will be late on the outs. In most cases, covers the #1 or #5 receiver man-to-man on any route of +10 yards.

Note: One problem associated with this coverage is that the quarter-coverage defender is asked to do too much: either covering the inside (#2 and #4) receivers at 12 to 15 yards and helping on the post or taking away the square-in routes by the #1 or #5 receiver yet being careful of the post. It is difficult for him to play aggressively.

Pattern #1

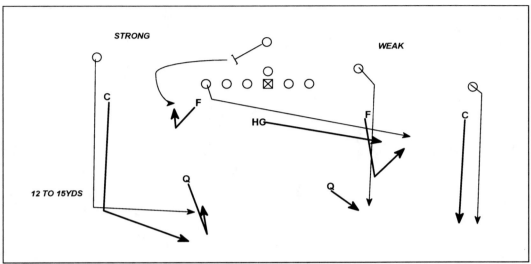

Diagram 9-2. Pattern #1

Strongside F: Covers the final #2 receiver man-to-man (outside portion of the #2 and #3 receivers).

HC: Covers the final #3 receiver across; either wall off or intersect the crosser (refer to Chapter 4, Diagrams 4-2 and 4-3).

Weakside F: Works from the inside to the outside portion of the seam by the #4 receiver; comes off any flat threat (e.g., the crosser).

Strongside Q: If short routes by the #2 and #3 receivers, covers any inside break by the #1 receiver aggressively.

Weakside Q: Must carry any seam by the #4 receiver with the inside technique.

Strongside C: With the inside break by the #1 receiver, stays on top, and expects the post; covers man-to-man.

Weakside Q: Covers the #5 receiver; covers man-to-man after 12 yards.

Pattern #2

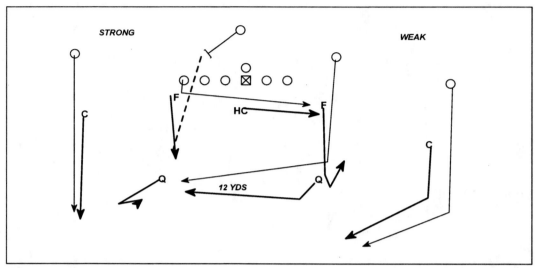

Diagram 9-3. Pattern #2

Strongside F: Stacks back on the final #2 receiver (the back); reads the quarterback, and must be alert for crossers or a checkdown by the #2 receiver.

HC: Covers the final #3 receiver man-to-man, and must be alert for him to hook up.

Weakside F: Covers the #4 receiver in the seam; when Q picks him up, the weakside F reads the quarterback (the crosser or under the #5 receiver).

Strongside Q: If short routes for the #2 and #3 receivers, helps cover the #1 receiver; if the #1 receiver is gone, looks for the crosser.

Weakside Q: If the #4 receiver works downfield, covers him.

Strongside C: Maintains inside leverage, and covers the #1 receiver man-to-man.

Weakside C: Maintains inside leverage, and covers the #5 receiver man-to-man.

Pattern #3

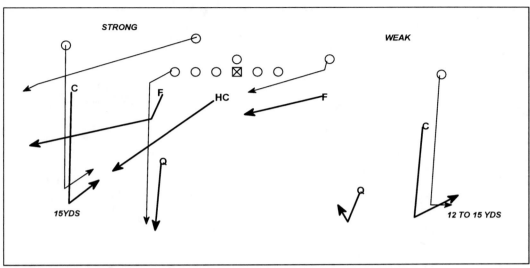

Diagram 9-4. Pattern #3

Strongside F: Works through the curl and then to the flat receiver (the back); must be alert for the break downfield second through the zone.

HC: Gets to the first inside breaker (the #1 or final #2 receiver); looks back to the quarterback when an arm's distance away. To be a factor in the coverage, does not drift.

Weakside F: If the #3 receiver is away, comes down on the #4 receiver by man-to-man coverage; has no one else to cover.

Strongside Q: Covers the seam.

Weakside Q: Reads the quarterback; has no one else to cover.

Strongside C: Covers the #1 receiver man-to-man once he works downfield.

Weakside C: Covers the #5 receiver man-to-man.

Pattern #4

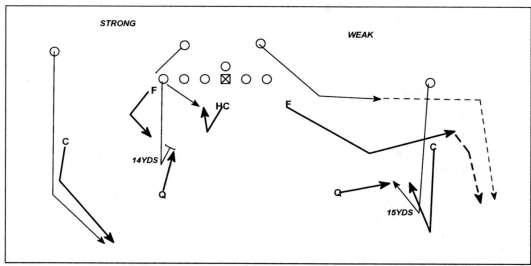

Diagram 9-5. Pattern #4. *Note*: This pattern is commonly used by offenses to defeat quarter coverage.

Strongside F: No outside portion of the #2 and #3 receiver; must be alert for the #1 receiver coming in.

HC: The final #3 receiver (the back on the trail route).

Weakside F: Works through the curl to the flat; must be alert for the second through the zone.

Strongside Q: Breaks to the #2 receiver with inside leverage; works a shoulder (refer to Chapter 3, Diagram 3-11).

Weakside Q: Breaks to the #5 receiver, and gets in front of him. The weakside C is on top.

Strongside C: Inside technique; takes away the post.

Weakside C: Covers the #5 receiver on top; could help on the back downfield if the deep break is early enough.

Pattern #5

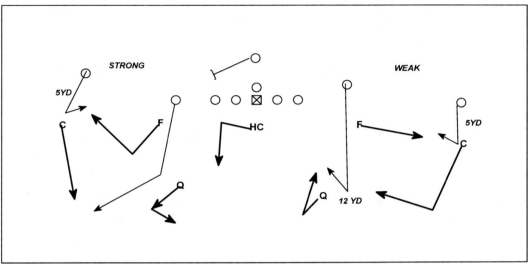

Diagram 9-6. Pattern #5

Strongside F: The route by the #1 receiver dictates the drive to this receiver; must be as wide as the widest receiver.

HC: Stacks on the #3 receiver; reads the quarterback, and finds the threat. Must be alert for a checkdown.

Weakside F: The route by the #5 receiver dictates the drive to him; must be wide as the widest receiver.

Strongside Q: Carries the #2 receiver when he is passed off to C; the strongside Q turns into the formation, and watches the crossers.

Weakside Q: Covers the hook of the #4 receiver.

Strongside C: Deep-quarter coverage (the #2 receiver on the corner route).

Weakside C: Deep-quarter coverage; if no threat, closes on the curl of the #4 receiver. Does not cover air.

Pattern #6

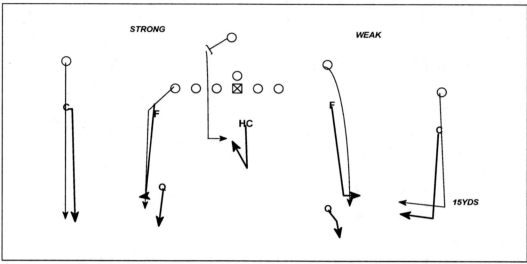

Diagram 9-7. Pattern #6

Strongside F: Works the outside portion of the seam by the #2 receiver. Watches the quarterback; must be alert to come off coverage at 15 yards, especially with a threat.

HC: Covers the #3 receiver; uses man-to-man coverage with no other reads.

Weakside F: Works to the outside portion of the seam by the #4 receiver. Looks for the quarterback; must be alert to come off coverage at 15 yards, especially with a threat.

Strongside Q: Carries the seam.

Weakside Q: Carries the seam.

Strongside C: Covers the #1 receiver man-to-man.

Weakside C: Covers the #5 receiver man-to-man inside after 15 yards.

Pattern #7

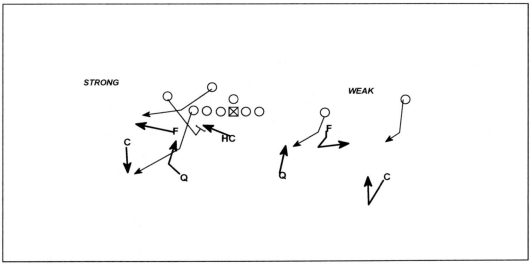

Diagram 9-8. Pattern #7

Strongside F: Flat.

HC: Covers the option route (the final #3 receiver).

Weakside F: Starts to come down with the #4 receiver (since the #3 receiver is away). With the Q in position, the weakside F comes off on the #5 receiver; must be aware this action happens in a split second.

Strongside Q: If the corner route is passed off to the C, comes down on the outside portion of the option.

Weakside Q: Covers inside the #4 receiver.

Strongside C: Covers the corner route (outside quarter).

Weakside C: Comes down on top of the #5 receiver.

Pattern #8 (Flow)

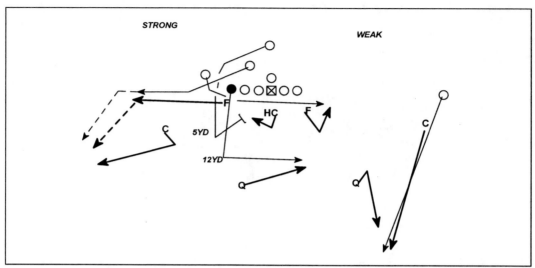

Diagram 9-9. Pattern #8 (flow)

Strongside F: Covers the flat; must be alert for the second through the zone. Stays on top.

HC: With flow, passes off first crosser to F; works to final #3 receiver.

Weakside F: If flow, takes the first crosser.

Strongside Q: Covers the square-in route (inside quarter). Performs a natural pickup.

Weakside Q: If no immediate threat, helps on the #5 receiver.

Strongside C: If nothing to cover, must be alert the flat is going deep.

Weakside C: Covers the #5 receiver deep.

Pattern #9 (Flow)

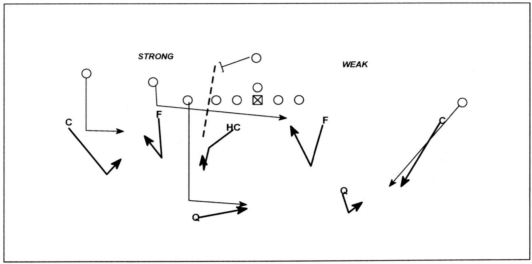

Diagram 9-10. Pattern #9 (flow)

Strongside F: Covers outside the #2 receiver and the #3 receiver from inside the #2 receiver; if they are gone, covers wide as the widest receiver (the #1 receiver).

HC: If flow, passes the first crosser to the weakside F; stacks back, and must be alert for a checkdown.

Weakside F: If flow, covers the first crosser high to low.

Strongside Q: Stays inside the square-in (final #2 receiver) route.

Weakside Q: Covers deepest receiver in the inside quarter (the #5 receiver).

Strongside C: Covers the outside quarter; if no threat, comes on the #1 receiver.

Weakside C: Covers the #5 receiver.

Pattern #10

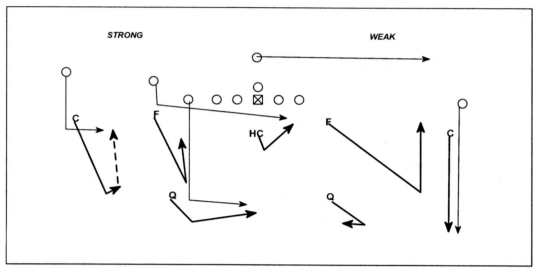

Diagram 9-11. Pattern #10

Strongside F: Covers the outside portion of the #2 and #3 receivers from the inside of the #2 receiver; if they are gone, helps under the final #2 or #1 receiver (must be as wide as the widest receiver).

HC: Covers the final #3 receiver (the low crosser); wall off or intersect (refer to Chapter 4, Diagrams 4-3 and 4-4).

Weakside F: Curls to the flat.

Strongside Q: Covers the square-in (final #2 receiver) route.

Weakside Q: Looks for the #5 receiver; if the #5 receiver is clear, he turns back to the formation, and watches the crosser.

Strongside C: Clears the outside quarter, and then comes down on the #1 receiver.

Weakside C: Covers the #5 receiver.

Pattern #11

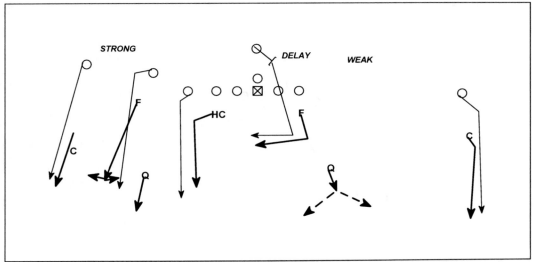

Diagram 9-12. Pattern #11. *Note:* The longer a key delays, the more man-to-man coverage by the defender.

Strongside F: Carries the seam by the #2 receiver for 15 yards, and then must be alert for breaking receivers in or out.

HC: Carries the #3 receiver down the seam; does not count on help because the situation is tough.

Weakside F: If the #4 receiver is the widest of the inside receivers, the weakside F covers him.

Strongside Q: Gets depth inside the #2 receiver and outside the #3 receiver; reads the quarterback.

Weakside Q: Looks for the #5 receiver; reads the quarterback, and tries to help the trips side.

Strongside C: Covers the #1 receiver.

Weakside C: Covers the #5 receiver.

Pattern #12 (Flow)

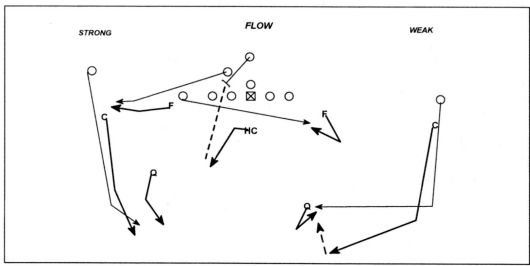

Diagram 9-13. Pattern #12 (flow)

Strongside F: Flat.

HC: Flow; passes off the first crosser (the weakside F has the first crosser). Stacks on the final #3 receiver (the back); must be alert for a checkdown.

Weakside F: If flow, covers the first open crosser.

Strongside Q: If the #2 and #3 receivers are short, gets to the #1 receiver; helps on the post.

Weakside Q: Has flow alert to cover the #5 receiver in the square-in route.

Strongside C: Covers the #1 receiver.

Weakside C: Protects the post by the #5 receiver, and then comes down on the #5 receiver.

10

Zone Dogs

Zone dogs are plays that include a zone and a blitz to attack certain protections or to overload an area. Zone dogs work nicely with pattern reading. They force defenders to match up to prevent large holes from opening in the zones. The most important aspect of zone dogs is the coverages that are used rather than the path of the blitzers. It is difficult to have success if the coverages in zone dogs change every week, especially when dropping defensive linemen who are not familiar with the coverage.

Rush Concepts

This book does not discuss fronts. However, the zone dog coverage is based on where the pressure is applied. Following are the seven ways to call zone dogs:

- Overload the tight end: Pressure comes from the tight end side regardless of the formation.
- Overload the openside: Pressure comes from the openside regardless of the formation.
- Overload the strongside: Pressure comes from the strongside, which usually is declared by where the two receivers align (i.e., tight end and wideout or two-wide-receiver side).
- Overload the weakside: Pressure comes away from the strongside.
- Overload the middle: This concept usually applies to any pressure inside the offensive tackles.

- Overload the directional: This concept is used if the defense wants to pressure a side (i.e., right or left because of personnel or right or left because of the wideside or shortside of the field).
- Outside the right and left off the edge: This concept comes from outside to both sides; favored versus perimeter runs or bootlegs should be used when the side it is going towards is not certain.

Issues in Zone Dogs

Zone dogs must be able to handle adjustments versus movement, one-back sets, and, most of all, empty sets. If these situations are not dealt with, offenses will have big opportunities to get receivers wide open due to a mismatch or an error because of confusion about formation or personnel. Another concern is that when pressuring on the snap of the ball, a run or a roll pass may occur away from the pressure. Pulling out of the pressure is easier said than done because, in reality, it may slow the pressure.

Zone Dog Coverages

Basically, the three zone coverages previously discussed work well with zone dogs because they match up to receivers. This book shows a few concepts of zone dogs that might be used without dropping any defensive lineman into coverage. The zone dogs are utilized in base defense and nickel and dime defenses.

4 Under 3 Deep (3 Under 3 Deep if No Down Lineman Drops Out): Strong, Tight End, or (Left) Directional Zone Dog

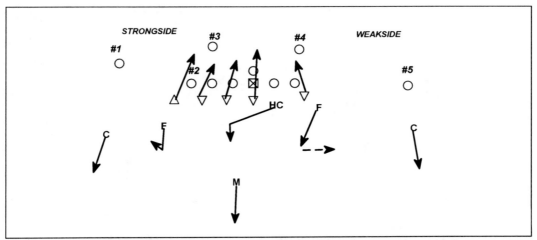

Diagram 10-1. 4 under 3 deep (3 under 3 deep if no down lineman drops out): strong, tight end, or (left) directional zone dog

Strongside and weakside Cs: Have outside one-third; cover the #1 and #5 receivers man-to-man on any route over 12 yards.

Strongside F: Holds the outside portion of the #2 and #3 receivers; does not go to the flat unless a receiver is in the flat or a receiver brings him to the flat. Must be alert to carry seams by the #2 or #3 receiver.

HC: Middle-hook drop; has the inside portion of the #2, #3, and #4 receivers. On the flow, lets the first crosser go to the weakside F.

Weakside F: Holds the outside portion of the #4 receiver; does not go to the flat unless a receiver is in the flat. Must be alert to carry the seam by the #4 receiver; on the flow, covers the first uncovered crosser.

M: Middle one-third.

4 Under 3 Deep (3 Under 3 Deep if No Down Lineman Drops Out): Weak, Open, or (Right) Directional Zone Dog

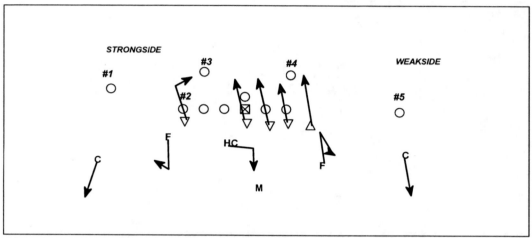

Diagram 10-2. 4 under 3 deep (3 under 3 deep if no down lineman drops out): weak, open, or (right) directional zone dog

Strongside and weakside Cs: Have outside one-third; cover the #1 and #5 receivers man-to-man on any route over 12 yards.

Strongside F: Holds the outside portion of the #2 or #3 receiver; does not go to the flat unless a receiver is in the flat or a receiver brings him to the flat. Must be alert to carry seams by the #2 or #3 receiver.

HC: Middle-hook drop; has the inside portion of the #2, #3, and #4 receivers. On the flow, lets the first crosser go to the weakside F.

Weakside F: Holds the outside portion of the #4 receiver; does not go to the flat unless a receiver is in the flat. Must be alert to carry the seam by the #4 receiver; on the flow, covers the first uncovered crosser.

M: Middle one-third.

5 Under 2 Deep (4 Under 2 Deep if No Lineman Drops Out): Right and Left Off-the-Edge Zone Dogs

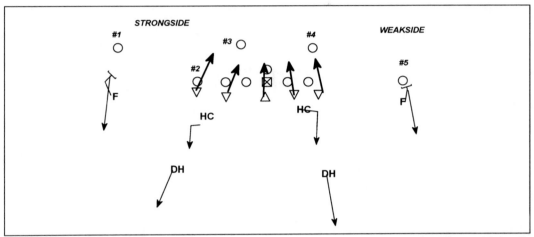

Diagram 10-3. 5 under 2 deep (4 under 2 deep if no lineman drops out): right and left off-the-edge zone dogs

No major changes occur in a two-back set (refer to Chapter 8) except that the strongside HC is inside the #2 and #3 receivers. He cannot cut to a receiver. He must stack back and watch the #2 and #3 receivers, covering the most dangerous receiver. The weakside HC must also stack on the #4 receiver. Hopefully, the #3 or #4 receiver will stay inside to block.

5 Under 2 Deep (4 Under 2 Deep if No Lineman Drops Out): Right and Left Off-the-Edge Zone Dogs

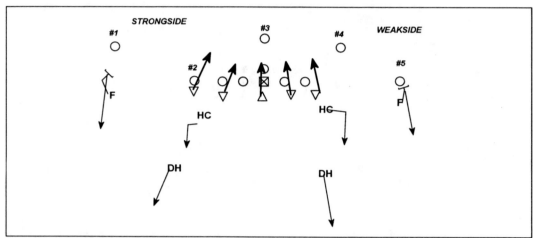

Diagram 10-4. 5 under 2 deep (4 under 2 deep if no lineman drops out): right and left off-the-edge zone dogs

No major changes occur in a two-back set (refer to Chapter 8) except that the strongside HC is inside the #2 and #3 receivers. He cannot cut to a receiver. He must stack back and watch the #2 and #3 receivers, covering the most dangerous receiver. In a one-back set that is 2-2, the strongside HC cannot carry the seam by the #2 receiver. He must come off the seam no deeper than 15 yards to help on the #3 receiver or any crossers. The strongside DH must be aware of this situation.

3 Under 4 Across—Quarters (2 Under 4 Across if No Lineman Drops Out): Middle-Zone Dog

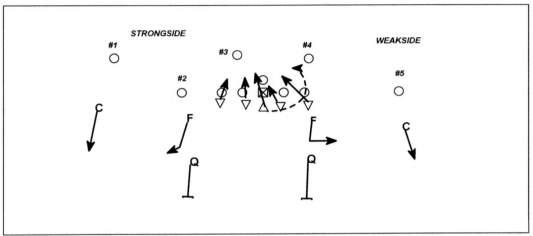

Diagram 10-5. 3 under 4 across—quarters (2 under 4 across if no lineman drops out): middle-zone dog

This coverage is played like 3 under 4 across—quarters coverage (refer to Chapter 9) except that Fs are responsible for the final #2, #3, and #4 receivers. Fs can only leave their stacked positions on the #2 and #4 receivers if the flats are threatened. Fs align inside the #2 and #4 receivers to have the ability to come down on them when the #3 receiver goes away.

3 Under 4 Across—Quarters (2 Under 4 Across if No Lineman Drops Out): Middle-Zone Dog

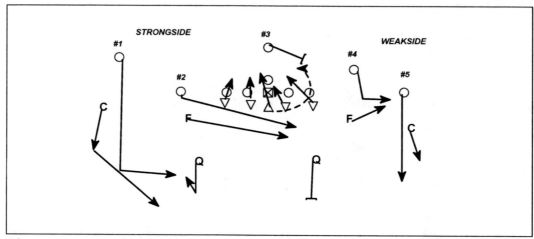

Diagram 10-6. 3 under 4 across—quarters (2 under 4 across if no lineman drops out): middle-zone dog

The diagram shows why Fs align inside (see strongside F). He comes down with the #2 receiver since the #3 receiver is gone. The weakside F is aligned inside but has outside responsibility; he will be a step late to the flat.

Defending Screens

Screens are reaction plays and, therefore, are difficult to practice. Sometimes, it is a good idea to run screens in practice with all zone coverages and without a defensive line to get the proper support lanes. When matching the zones in pattern reading, it occasionally helps to take stack defenders who are stacked on a back and "engage" the back. This technique can give a team a head start against an opponent that uses screens frequently.

General Coaching Points

The defender must "stay alive" unless he is making a commitment to a tackle; he should use his hands and do everything he can to keep on his feet, to ensure he will not have to take on an offensive lineman in open space. Proper angles to the screen are critical. The basic rule in all screens is that players should not get behind players in their own jerseys. In other words, when a defender is running to the screen, he should take a different lane than his teammate is running in (Diagram 11-1).

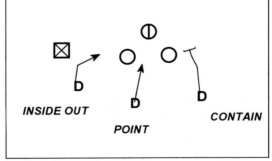

Diagram 11-1. Ideal screen defense. Linebackers have the best chance to see "sliding linemen" to the screen. If a window opens up, it sometimes is best for the first defender to take his shot.

Support Patterns and Angles

Usually the flat defender will take the outside contain position. The second defender to the screen must maintain the inside approach. If he has help behind him, he can be the "point man." According to a two-year study conducted by me and my staff to find out the reason we were having trouble with screens, the main cause of a big gain on a screen was that the second man to the screen lost the inside-out approach and overran the play. The alley between the contain defender and the inside defender must be squeezed (Diagram 11-2).

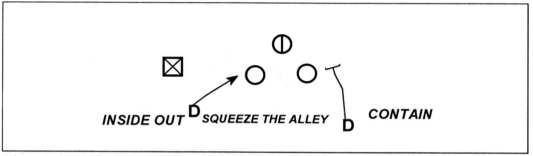

Diagram 11-2. Alley between the contain defender and the inside defender. *Note:* Usually, the point man is missing.

Fake Screen

When screens are played well or if they are overplayed, the back will change his path and redirect away from the sliding linemen. Many times this play is a called "fake" (Diagram 11-3). To defend a fake screen, the defender cannot lose sight of the back when he reacts to the sliding linemen. He must maintain leverage on the back (Diagram 11-4).

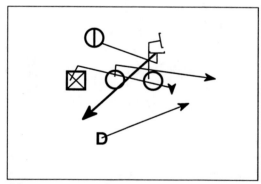

Diagram 11-3. Fake screen

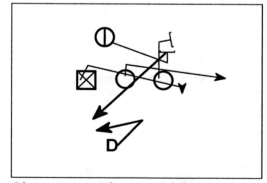

Diagram 11-4. Fake screen defense

Quick Screen to the Wideout (or Any Receiver Aligned in the Wideout Position)

A quick screen is basically a perimeter run play. The defense must have a contain man—an inside alley defender. When a defense does not put someone in alignment with the #2 or #4 receiver, they are removed from the formation (Diagram 11-5), which immediately puts the defense at a disadvantage by alignment. The starting point for defending this screen is the ability of the defensive end to handle "chop" blocking by the offensive tackle. If the defensive end can protect his legs and get in the quarterback's throwing lane, he can be a major factor in defending the play. The defense must have someone in the inside run alley and another defender on an outside-in contain position to prevent the receiver from getting in the inside alley. The defense must disrupt his path downfield and force him to go sideways (Diagram 11-6). Many times, these screens are executed from one-back or empty sets. It is the offense's way of getting a perimeter run from an empty set without movement.

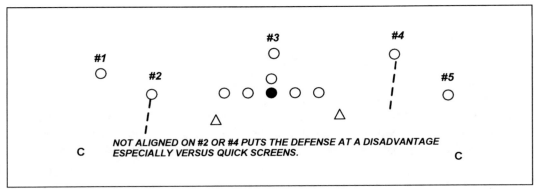

Diagram 11-5. Quick screen

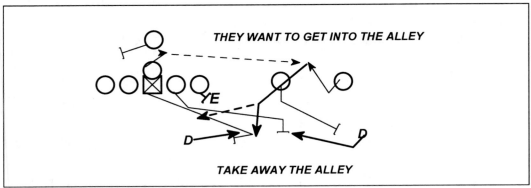

Diagram 11-6. Quick screen defense

12

Additional Important Defensive Points

Disguising

Disadvantages

Most defensive systems try to disguise the fronts and coverage so that the offense will not gain a pre-snap read. The principle of disguising is sound; however, problems do occur when defenses disguise. Following are some disadvantages of defensive disguising:

- Defenders have a tendency to lose sight of their keys. Defenders must move around, but they still must pick up their keys. Sometimes, movement makes players lose focus on their keys.
- During movement, defenders occasionally are caught out of position and cannot get back to their position to make the play (Diagram 12-1).
- Sometimes, technique is sacrificed with the time put into disguising.

Advantages

Defensive disguising has advantages as long as it is coordinated and not jumbled. Following are some advantages of defensive disguising:

- It can completely take away pre-snap reads, limiting what the offense might automatic.
- It can encourage the offense to call a play that will be directed to the strength of a defense (Diagram 12-2).

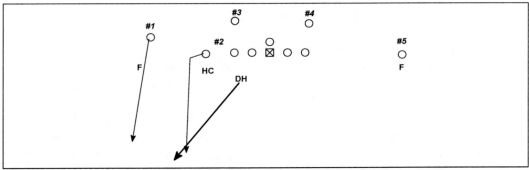

Diagram 12-1. The deep-half defender is disguising the blitz or an eight-man front (5 under 2 deep). The ball is snapped quickly, and he is totally out of position. He must turn and run to have any chance in the coverage.

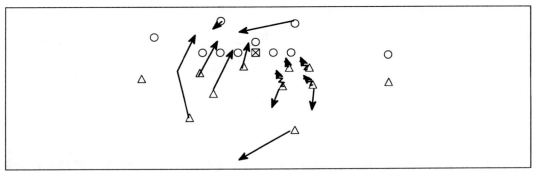

Diagram 12-2. The defense shows an overload to the defensive right side, and the quarterback automatically throws to the other side where the blitz is actually happening—the defensive left side.

- When an offense expects pressure, it can invite a "sight adjustment" or a blitz adjustment. Most offenses change adjustments from week to week. However, defensively, if the adjustments are discovered, it is worth the attempt to invite the throw (Diagram 12-3).

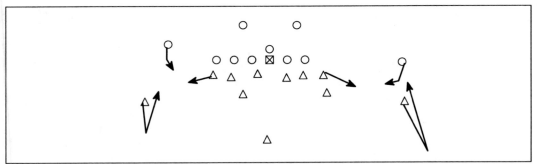

Diagram 12-3. The defense shows the blitz, knowing that the slant to the wideouts is a blitz adjustment. The defense drives the outside defenders under the outside receivers with the defensive backs on top

The No-Cover Zone

The no-cover zone is the area from the line of scrimmage to about five yards downfield. Many zone teams have a no-cover zone to allow crossers to be passed off to another defender. In addition, no-cover zones are used to assure depth in the drops by underneath defenders. This zone can also be used in the early teaching of the pattern reading system. However, it defeats the purpose in many cases and takes away the ability to close the zone areas of the zone defense. If seams are carried, then someone must cover crossers. It is also difficult to take away throwing lanes. Picking up routes is a more aggressive way to play zone coverages (Diagrams 12-4 to 12-6).

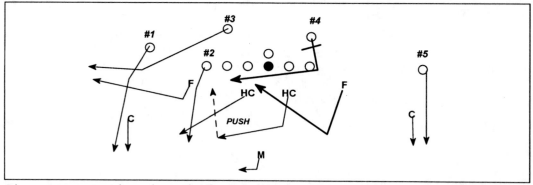

Diagram 12-4. 4 under 3 deep. The flat defender must come down on the #4 receiver. A basic rule in pattern reading is that when a key blocks and then releases the defender responsible for him must cover him man-to-man (or the longer the defender's key blocks the more man-to-man coverage is needed after the stack drop).

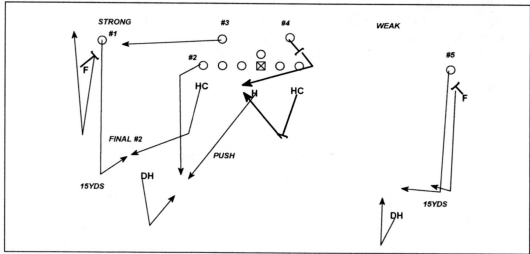

Diagram 12-5. 5 under 2 deep. The weakside hook/curl defender must come down on the #4 defender.

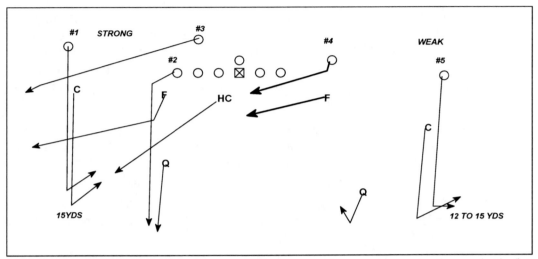

Diagram 12-6. 3 under 4 across—quarters. This coverage is one reason why the weakside flat defender must align inside, even though someone brings him to the flat. Everyone is gone; therefore, he must come down with the #4 receiver.

Crossers in the Backfield

When receivers cross behind the line of scrimmage, they are counted. Usually, these receivers are backs, but with today's formations, they could be any type of receiver in the backfield (Diagram 12-7).

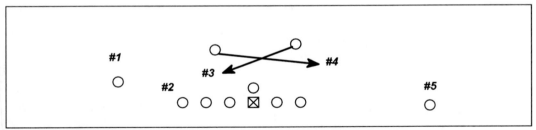

Diagram 12-7. Crossers in the backfield

Teaching Progression

Following are the six key elements of teaching progression for any position, especially the coverage aspect of any defense:

- Responsibility: What is the defender trying to defend? Occasionally, it is not clear to the player. Coaches sometimes teach the skills before telling players what they are attempting to defend.

- Stance and alignment: How many times have you seen a bad or wrong alignment put a player in a position that success is made difficult? Good stance in any position should be studied and fit into the technique you are trying to use. A stance is specific to your defense and what must be accomplished in the total defense.
- Keys and reaction: In every defense, a player should have a key and a reaction to that key.
- Initial movement: What are the first two or three steps? When a player is a step late to being successful on a given play, many times he lost a step in his initial movement. He becomes a player who "almost" makes plays.
- Technique: The technique the coach is asking the player to execute. .
- Finish: Finish is about making the play. Do players make the play (by tackling, passing, etc.)? In other words, do they have the X factor? Doing everything correctly isn't enough; players must *finish* every play.

Out of the Quarterback's Vision

Interceptions occur when a defender is out of the quarterback's vision. In pattern reading, a stack defender usually has a chance to see the quarterback across the formation and break on the throw (Diagram 12-8).

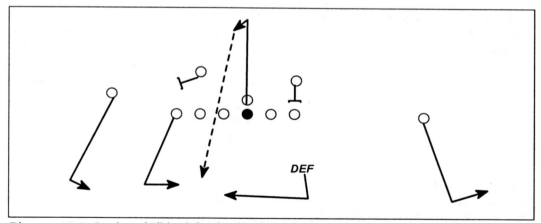

Diagram 12-8. Stack and slide defender (DEF) reads the quarterback's throw

Jamming Receivers

Jamming a receiver is a critical part of any coverage because it disrupts the timing of the route. It is a great advantage in college football because the jam on the receiver can be done downfield no matter how deep the receiver is as long as the ball is not in the air. Jamming in zones is done not only to disrupt the timing but also to restrict the size of the zone (Diagram 12-9).

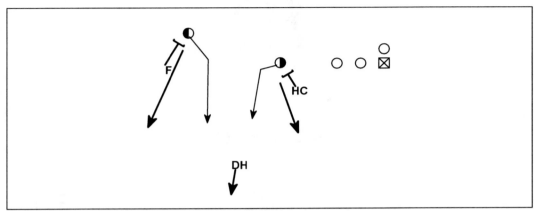

Diagram 12-9. Example of 5 under 2 deep jams. The jams by the flat defender and the hook/curl defender squeeze the area for the deep-half defender to cover. The flat defender jams the widest receiver inside from an outside leverage position. The hook/curl defender jams the inside receiver outside from inside leverage.

Rerouting Receivers

Rerouting a receiver means the defender will get in his path downfield and attempt to change his path without contacting him. In the NFL, this technique is the only one that can be used legally after five yards (Diagram 12-10).

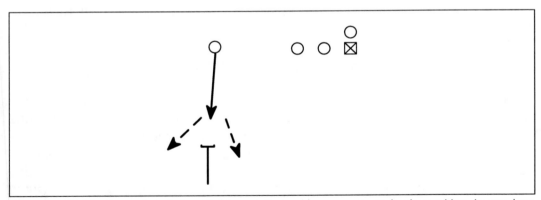

Diagram 12-10. Example of downfield rerouting with no contact; body position is used to disrupt the timing.

13

Problems

Every defense has problems and weaknesses. Knowing defensive problems is one of the coach's main responsibilities. Sometimes, the holes in a given defense can only be corrected by calling a different defense. A perfect defense does not exist; offenses always find ways to attack every defense. This chapter discusses common problems that occur when matching up patterns, as well as the difficulties of teaching this defense.

Problems in Teaching

If staff members, including the head coach, do not believe in the philosophy of patter reading pass defense, then coaching it will be extremely difficult, because early in the installation it may not look "pretty." Once the players know the concepts, this defense will be the only way they will want to play, because it gives them a better chance to cover receivers and break to the throw. Many of the defensive patterns previously discussed in this book did not come from a coach; they came from players who figured out things on their own to help them get to receivers faster.

Another reason the staff must believe in the philosophy is to ensure they give players corrections that are consistent with the defensive philosophy. For example, many coaches have been trained to teach players to never take their eyes off the quarterback. However, one of the rules in this defense is that defenders need to maintain sight on the receiver and may take their eyes off the quarterback to do so. Therefore, coaches must believe in the philosophy and understand its special rules to accurately teach and correct players. An effective way to demonstrate to coaches and players the value of maintaining sight on the receiver (instead of the quarterback) is to show them tapes of any game and count how many passes are completed because the defender loses sight of the receiver or cannot find the receiver.

Seam Issues

In the "deep in" by the outside receiver with the inside receiver running the seam, the #3 receiver goes away (Diagram 13-1). To correct this problem, the inside defender must be aware of the route. Using the eyes and body technique (Diagram 13-2), the body takes away the seam, but the eyes are outside. When the outside receiver breaks the route off, the inside defender goes to the receiver.

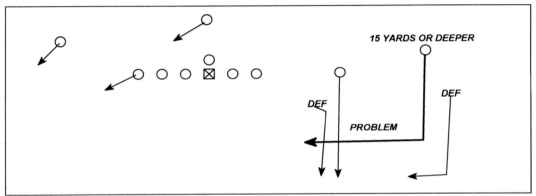

Diagram 13-1. The outside receiver has a chance to get open. Notice that the #3 receiver is away from the pattern. If the #3 receiver is to the side of the route, it puts an extra defender on the play.

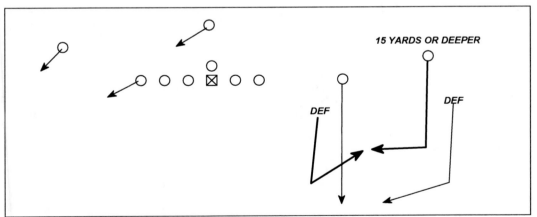

Diagram 13-2. Eyes and body technique. *Note:* Making the defender aware of the problem is half the battle.

Crosser Issues

Picking up crossing receivers must be sound in any defense. However, in a pattern match-up, it is critical because, on the other side of the formation, the defenders are aggressively picking up the patterns (Diagram 13-3). When dealing with crossers in any of the matched-up coverages, a simple rule can apply to all coverages. The defender responsible for the #3 receiver must cover the low crosser (i.e., the final #3 receiver) if the #3 receiver steps to the low crosser (Diagram 13-4) or goes across a trips formation (Diagram 13-5). The defender may use the wall-off or intersect technique (refer to Chapter 4, Diagrams 4-2 and 4-3). When the #3 receiver steps away from the low crosser, the defender will have to cover him, based on the coverage called (Diagrams 13-6 and 13-7).

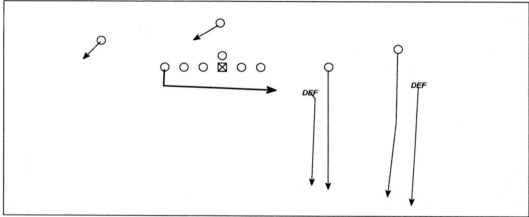

Diagram 13-3. The crosser must always be accounted for.

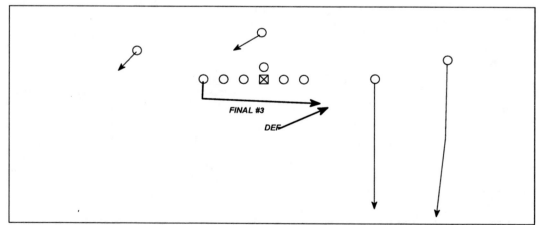

Diagram 13-4.The #3 receiver steps to the low crosser. The defender is responsible for the final #3 receiver.

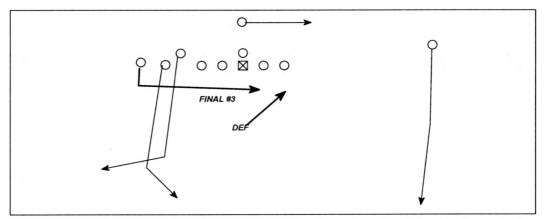

Diagram 13-5. The #3 receiver goes across the trips formation. The defender shown in the diagram is responsible for the final #3 receiver

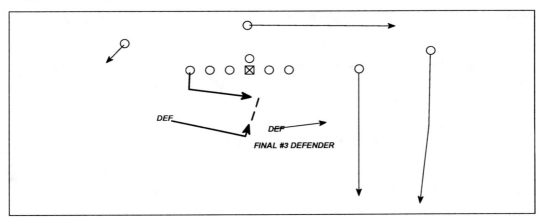

Diagram 13-6. The defender for the #3 receiver is gone (example 1). The next defender must be alert to come down with the next receiver.

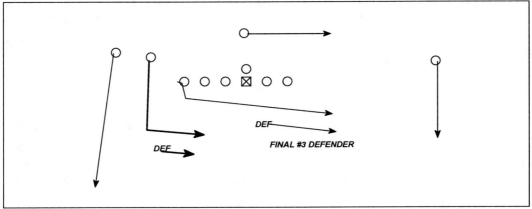

Diagram 13-7. The defender for the #3 receiver is gone (example 2). The next defender must be alert to come down with the next receiver.

Appendix A:
Principles and Coaching Practices

The results you get from your players must translate into wins. You can get anyone to work hard, but results count the most. To achieve the desired result, you must begin with the end in mind, such as the Super Bowl.

Before getting on the right path, you must find out how many snaps will occur in practice each week (e.g., 105 to 150). When you know this number, you can gauge how much you can install. You must know what is needed to win the big one.

Sometimes, strategy is overrated, especially on defense. Television announcers make it seem like the key to success is just putting players in certain positions and/or alignments. Success takes more, including hard technical coaching during the week and execution of those techniques on game day.

Teaching in the Classroom

You must realize that what you teach in an air-conditioned classroom does not always translate to the field. Those great ideas inside are not always so great outside.

During the first meeting, you should tell the players what is expected, the rules, and the team's goal. The coach's job is to bring players beyond what they think they can do, making them better than they think they can be. To this end, you must tell them why you correct them on the field so that they will take the coaching. Your job is to coach to reach perfection with the realization that it cannot be reached. Finally, you should assume nothing. For example, when I was a high school coach, I had a good free safety. When he graduated, he asked me what I really meant by cover the deep one-third. That instance was an awakening for me.

Tell your players to forget the scoreboard and think about playing (i.e., winning). They must understand the meaning of pursuit ("running to the ball when you don't think you can get there") or that making two extra plays a game might turn the game in their favor. Players must want to pursue. A coach must give them a "want-to" attitude.

Organize Yourself in the Classroom

As a coach, you must know all you can about a given technique (stance, alignments, initial movement, and responsibilities) so you can correct the errors that occur; however, if you try to teach every part of the technique in the classroom, you will lose the players. Organize your classroom procedure every day to make sure you cover all the important issues (and only those issues) and do not get off-topic.

Maintain Interest

In the classroom, you should not talk too long. When talking, change your pitch and ask questions (even make an obvious wrong statement and see the reaction); ask the players to repeat what you said. You should never lecture like a college professor. It might make you feel good, but the players may not be learning. In the NFL, players are in season for at least seven months with one to two hours of meetings every day; some players have heard the same thing for four or five years. It is tough for them to pay attention for more than one hour. Coaches who move around the room and use videos help make classroom learning more enjoyable for their players.

Lazy Mind

You must keep players' interest so that they do not get lazy. Sometimes, a player is smart enough but only hears one-half of what is said. His mind is "lazy." It is the coach's job to get a player's mind working.

Repeat, Repeat, Repeat

Occasionally, coaches get bored with repeating things, but repetition is a must in coaching. Repetition helps to ensure that players have "A" and "B" performance grades.

Corrections on Tapes

When correcting a player on tape, correct the performance and not the performer (unless he is loafing). When you correct a player, you must do so in such a way that he will *want* to do what you're asking him to do. If you correct him using fear or intimidation, he will be less likely to remember the correction or to apply it in the long term.

Sell What You Are Doing

You must sell what you are teaching and tell the players why they are doing what they are doing. This instruction must be done in the classroom. You should tell them how it will help them succeed at their position or how it will help the defense or offense succeed as a team. The higher the level of football, the more you must sell what you are doing. You must believe it also.

Whole/Part

Sometimes, it is better to play a short cut-up of what you want to coach before you discuss it. Many players need to get a picture of what the coach will talk about that day. This strategy can help players visualize what the coach is coaching.

Field Coaching and Practice

The difference between being a good teacher and being a good coach is the ability to recognize errors and correct them immediately (on the move). You must get the player to do what you want and do it with a one-week deadline. A coach must be a good teacher but must go one step further and coach the player beyond the mental aspect of the information.

Field Correction

Field corrections must be short and to the point. Discussion on the field must be limited. An NFL and college trick is for players to ask a question when they are tired to slow things down. Questions, not problems, should be answered. Remember, you are coaching to beat the best, which is why you must know all about a technique or scheme to correct it. Occasionally, coaches let poor technique slide with a good player. But ask yourself: "Is what he is doing going to beat the best teams you will face?" Only you can answer that question. Finally, a major problem at high levels of play is a tendency to coach players where to go but not tell them how to get there.

Field Organization

You should plan practice in advance, rather than planning drills on the way to the practice field. When you step on the field, you must have every minute of practice organized, including stretching, pre-practice, and postpractice, so that no time is wasted from the moment the players step on the field until the moment they step off the field.

Practice

Practice is where you check a player's honesty and character. His attitude and effort in practice will reveal many things about him; "attitude" refers to much more than just being polite, which has nothing to do with results. Never allow a player's personality to influence any decision that must be made by you, the coach; many nice guys are just not good enough players. Practice and game tapes also reveal a player's character. Is he putting the effort in practice? Some players believe they can just turn it on at game time, but they cannot. They must practice at full effort to ensure every step becomes a natural reaction, not a thought process. Many good players deteriorate rapidly as they get older because they have bad practice habits.

The X Factor

Players who make plays (like the player who has that last six-inch pop to explode on contact or the player who can "slip and slide" away from a blocker and make the play) instead of *almost* making plays have the X factor. The X factor cannot be taught; it is inside a player.

Coaching Evaluation

Remember, a player will evaluate you based on how much you teach him, how well you present it, and how quickly he can learn it. You also are evaluated on how you treat substitutions; it tells players what kind of person you are. You do not have to be liked, but you must be respected to the point that players will listen and do what you teach. A coach will be remembered by how he makes a player feel about himself.

Evaluation of Players

Position Competition

Nothing motivates players like position competition: the possibility of one player taking a position from another player. The higher the level of play, the higher the pride and competitiveness.

Maintaining Intensity

It is important to maintain intensity throughout a season. During a long season, complacency often sets in, and even you, the coach, do not realize it. Complacency affects players' performances. It can be seen on cut-ups after the season: a deterioration of details in technique that puts players a step away from a play. Coaches often ask themselves how they let this situation happen and become distracted with where a player should be instead of how he should get there. Instead, coaches should focus on maintaining intensity in themselves and their players, and ensure that players always use proper technique.

Player Evaluation

A player must know that he will be evaluated on every play, especially in a game. Coaches must be sold on this concept because it takes a long time to evaluate (grade) a tape. These evaluations also let a coach know if he is doing a good job teaching when he can look at tapes with his players and ask them to tell him what they did wrong and correct it themselves.

Great Athlete Syndrome

Do not fall into the trap of playing the great athlete with potential (jumps high, runs fast, etc.) who does not have the X factor. The most productive players should play. Young players need opportunities to play in games, but you should not play them at the expense of winning. After all, if your team loses too many times, you might not still be coaching. It is not enough to have a "good program" if it does not win consistently; no one in administration will fight for you to keep your job over the long term. If physical attributes are equal between two players, then attitude is the deciding factor (team chemistry) on which player will play in the game.

Game Planning

Keep It Simple

Your game plan must be just right: it must include enough plays to handle all likely situations, but it must not include more than your players are capable of. To that end, it must be simple, but not so simple that you are unprepared for a particular game situation. In addition, having too much in a game plan can make players' technique suffer, and not enough may be an insult to some players' intelligence.

Mistakes

The two most common mistakes coaches make during a game in regard to the game plan are leaving it too soon and leaving it too late. The worst mistake is adding something on the sideline that has not been practiced. You cannot evaluate how something you add on the sideline takes away from your basic scheme.

When to Add

Do not add something to the game plan after Thursday practice for a Sunday game. It does not allow enough time to discover any potential problems with the new play, and, therefore, problems will likely occur during the game. Also, late additions are not fair to players.

Game Day

Pre-game

During the pre-game meeting, try to make sure the players are emotionally ready for the game. Be careful not to simply reflect how you feel. It is important to focus on how the team feels.

During the Game

On the sideline during the game, you should only make corrections within the confines of your scheme. It is preferable to give corrections to individual players, but if it is a team issue, then all players must be involved in the discussion of the correction. It is very difficult to get a good view of the action from the sideline; therefore, the press box coaches play a critical role in helping a coach on the sideline with the details of what is happening on the field. It is necessary to have a standard procedure for reviewing diagrams, notes, etc. with the team on the sideline between plays. It can mean the difference between winning and losing.

Halftime

Halftime should be organized with a purpose; corrections should be addressed in a specific manner. Adjustments must be made within the confines of the defensive scheme in the plan. Occasionally, the only problem is missed tackles, which should be addressed. Do not expect to make miraculous adjustments at halftime; instead, focus on making simple corrections or giving the team a new mind-set.

Motivation

Motivation is probably one of the most talked about topics in regard to winning and losing. Motivation does not occur from outside in, but from inside out. A person must have a personal, intrinsic ability to motivate himself. A coach can only hit that person's "hot" button to motivate him. It cannot be done on a one-time basis. It must be instilled long before the actual event takes place (i.e., inside out). It must be worked on year-round. It is not a one-time action.

Pep talks only work if a motivated person only needs a reminder to do what is necessary to win. Pep talks do not work if a person is not self-motivated. It may work for a few plays, but in the long term it must be inside a person.

In order for a self-motivated person to maintain his enthusiasm, he should have a respect for the information being taught, a respect for the person teaching, and a belief that it is possible to succeed. However, even if two of the three aforementioned are missing, the self-motivated player may still do what is necessary to win. The motivated player does not need someone to lead him. He leads himself.

When someone is motivated, it is not a one-time thing. It is something that has been cultivated on a long-term basis. Motivation must be established long before a pep talk on the sideline. It is necessary to have a long-term plan to motivate year-round.

For a player to feel motivated, he must also feel he is prepared to compete. He must feel he is physically and mentally prepared by his coach to the best of his ability. It is almost impossible to make a bad player good, but it is more than possible to make a good player better. (It is also possible to make a good player bad. Sometimes, the secret to coaching is getting some good players and not messing them up.)

It is difficult to judge or evaluate motivation. Looking at films to evaluate a player's effort is one way to determine his motivation during an event. However, only the player truly knows if he is giving his all.

Motivation from newspaper clippings, sayings, etc. only works on motivated people. To motivate a nonmotivated person is difficult, and the best motivator for those players is "position competition," as discussed previously.

It is a lot easier to motivate a player if he respects your teaching, your method, and the knowledge you give him that he could not get himself. A coach will be remembered by how he makes a person feel about himself, not the words he says, which will be forgotten.

Appendix B: Excuses

In the course of a season, a coach will hear a multitude of excuses from players. To help minimize excuses, coaches can use an excuse board. Every player's excuse should be added to the board. When a player makes an excuse, the coaching staff should refer to the board to see if it has been used previously or if it should be added. The excuse board is a fun way to remind players that excuses are not acceptable and that they will be held accountable when they make an excuse. Following are lists of common excuses.

Being Late

- I had to get taped.
- I had the wrong day or time to lift.
- The trainer was talking to me.
- The clock downstairs was wrong.
- I was getting treatment.
- I had to go to the bathroom.
- I came out of the game late so I didn't see personnel.
- The coach sent me in too late for the game.
- My clock was wrong because I didn't change the time.
- The bubble on the glass of my watch blocked the time.
- I was signing footballs.
- I didn't get a wake-up call.
- The showers were crowded.
- The coach talked too much.
- I fell a sleep because of the medication I took.
- I was talking to the head coach (when actually the head coach was in the back of the room).

Assignment and Mental Errors

- You never told me that.
- We didn't do that in practice.

- I slipped.
- I missed the call because I couldn't see the signal.
- I was aligned wrong because I was disguising.
- I was out of position because I was baiting him.
- I was moving to make the play so I aligned wrong.
- I never saw that before.
- I was playing it like last week.
- I didn't make the play because I didn't want to hit him in practice.
- I was in the wrong gap because I discussed it with the nose tackle.
- He "messed up"; not me.
- I didn't get the call.
- I thought I was the Mike linebacker as opposed to the Will linebacker.
- I blitzed the wrong way because I thought I was the dime (but he was the nickel).
- He screwed me up when he went offside.
- I didn't get enough repetitions.
- I saw him make a mistake, and I was covering up.
- The coach didn't tell me what it meant.
- It didn't look like my man.
- I missed the call because he distracted me.
- I couldn't make the play because water got in my eye.
- I couldn't separate from the blocker because my biceps are too big.
- I missed the interception because I missed the timing of my jump.
- I was hurt and couldn't make the play.
- The coach gave me the wrong personnel.
- I counted the center like the #3 receiver in the pattern (7/7 drill).
- I couldn't talk to him because my chin strap was in my mouth.
- I couldn't catch the ball because my thumbs were taped.
- The receiver ran by me because the technique you taught me doesn't work.
- I couldn't see because my helmet is too big.
- I played bad because I was hurt.

Whining

- They (scout team) didn't give a good picture.
- It wasn't me; it was him "man."
- The scout report has too many pages.

Lack of Effort

- My flat feet hurt.
- I couldn't run because my new shoes hurt.
- He blocked me because he had the angle on me.
- He outran me because he had the angle.
- I'm too tired today because I worked too hard yesterday.
- I didn't run to the ball because I didn't want to get around the pile.
- I was "sluggish" early in practice.
- I was not stretched enough to work too hard.
- I'll run to the ball tomorrow.
- I threw up because I ate ginseng for breakfast.
- I couldn't see because I had contact solution in my eye.
- I had five IVs one week ago that made me put on weight.
- I stopped running to the ball because I thought he would cut me.
- I faded (slept) a little because I worked too hard.
- I can't do much at practice today because I got stabbed last night.

Miscellaneous

- I was thinking like you "guys" (coaches told him something).
- I was on the ground resting to try to keep my back loose.
- I didn't know which meeting to go to today.
- I forgot I had my cell phone with me, I forgot to shut my cell phone off, or that can't be my cell phone.
- We didn't practice that drill.
- I was in the wrong room because I sleep walk; ask my parents.
- I didn't pull his jersey; it got caught on my Velcro (called for holding).
- My face mask got caught in his face mask.
- I left the meeting because my stomach was bubbling.
- I couldn't see the personnel because they were all "mushed" together on the sideline.

About the Author

Tom Olivadotti has coached every level of football (high school, college, and professional) in his 40-year career. He worked with the Houston Texans under Dom Capers (2004 to 2005), New York Giants under Jim Fassel (2000 to 2003), Minnesota Vikings under Denny Green (1996 to 1999), Miami Dolphins under Don Shula (1987 to 1995), and Cleveland Browns under Marty Schottenher (1985 to 1986) in various positions, including defensive coordinator, linebackers' coach, and defensive backs' coach. His NFL career highlights include the 2000 Super Bowl (New York Giants), 12 NFL playoff appearances, six division titles, and one conference title. During his 21 years in the NFL, his teams compiled an overall record of 177-126.

A graduate of Upsala College, where he played four years each of varsity football and baseball, Olivadotti began his career as a head high school coach, winning a state championship. He later worked as a linebackers' coach and defensive coordinator at the college level, including a stint with the University of Miami, which won the 1983 Division I-A National Championship during his tenure.

Several of the NFL players he worked with were selected to the Pro Bowl, and 18 of his University of Miami players were eventually drafted by NFL teams.